Best Climbs
Los Angeles

D1604455

Best Climbs
Los Angeles

Best Climbs
Los Angeles

DAMON CORSO

FALCONGUIDES

GUILFORD, CONNECTICUT
HELENA, MONTANA

AN IMPRINT OF ROWMAN & LITTLEFIELD

FALCONGUIDES®

An imprint of Rowman & Littlefield
Falcon, FalconGuides, and Outfit Your Mind are registered trademarks of Rowman & Littlefield.
Distributed by NATIONAL BOOK NETWORK

Copyright © 2015 by Rowman & Littlefield
Interior photos by Damon Corso.
Maps: Melissa Baker © Rowman & Littlefield
Topos: Sue Murray © Rowman & Littlefield

British Library Cataloguing-in-Publication Information available

Library of Congress Cataloging-in-Publication Data available
ISBN 978-0-7627-9632-8 (paperback)

∞™ The paper used in this publication meets the minimum requirements of American National Standard for Information Sciences—Permanence of Paper for Printed Library Materials, ANSI/NISO Z39.48-1992.

WARNING

Climbing is a sport where you may be seriously injured or die. Read this before you use this book.

This guidebook is a compilation of unverified information gathered from many different climbers. The author cannot ensure the accuracy of any of the information in this book, including the topos and route descriptions, the difficulty ratings, and the protection ratings. These may be incorrect or misleading, as ratings of climbing difficulty and danger are always subjective and depend on the physical characteristics (for example, height), experience, technical ability, confidence, and physical fitness of the climber who supplied the rating. Additionally, climbers who achieve first ascents sometimes underrate the difficulty or danger of the climbing route. Therefore, be warned that you must exercise your own judgment on where a climbing route goes, its difficulty, and your ability to safely protect yourself from the risks of rock climbing. Examples of some of these risks are: falling due to technical difficulty or due to natural hazards such as holds breaking, falling rock, climbing equipment dropped by other climbers, hazards of weather and lightning, your own equipment failure, and failure or absence of fixed protection.

You should not depend on any information gleaned from this book for your personal safety; your safety depends on your own good judgment, based on experience and a realistic assessment of your climbing ability. If you have any doubt as to your ability to safely climb a route described in this book, do not attempt it.

The following are some ways to make your use of this book safer:

1. Consultation: You should consult with other climbers about the difficulty and danger of a particular climb prior to attempting it. Most local climbers are glad to give advice on routes in their area; we suggest that you contact locals to confirm ratings and safety of particular routes and to obtain firsthand information about a route chosen from this book.

2. Instruction: Los Angeles County has a strong community of local climbing instructors and guides available; a list is available in the appendix. We recommend that you engage an instructor or guide to learn safety techniques and to become familiar with the routes and hazards of the areas described in this book. Even after you are proficient in climbing safely, occasional use of a guide is a safe way to raise your climbing standard and learn advanced techniques.

3. Fixed Protection: Some of the routes in this book may use bolts and pitons that are permanently placed in the rock. Because of variances in the manner of placement, weathering, metal fatigue, the quality of the metal used, and many other factors, these fixed protection pieces should always be considered suspect and should always be backed up by equipment that you place yourself. Never depend on a single piece of fixed protection for your safety, because you never can tell whether it will hold weight. In some cases, fixed protection may have been removed or is now missing. However, climbers should not always add new pieces of protection unless existing protection is faulty. Existing protection can be tested by an experienced climber and its strength determined. Climbers are strongly encouraged not to add bolts and drilled pitons to a route. They need to climb the route in the style of the first ascent party (or better) or choose a route within their ability—a route to which they do not have to add additional fixed anchors.

Be aware of the following specific potential hazards that could arise in using this book:

1. Incorrect Descriptions of Routes: If you climb a route and you have a doubt as to where it goes, you should not continue unless you are sure that you can go that way safely. Route descriptions and topos in this book could be inaccurate or misleading.

2. Incorrect Difficulty Rating: A route might be more difficult than the rating indicates. Do not be lulled into a false sense of security by the difficulty rating.

3. Incorrect Protection Rating: If you climb a route and you are unable to arrange adequate protection from the risk of falling through the use of fixed pitons or bolts and by placing your own protection devices, do not assume that there is adequate protection available higher just because the route protection rating indicates the route does not have an X or an R rating. Every route is potentially an X (a fall may be deadly), due to the inherent hazards of climbing—including, for example, failure or absence of fixed protection, your own equipment's failure, or improper use of climbing equipment.

There are no warranties, whether expressed or implied, that this guidebook is accurate or that the information contained in it is reliable. There are no warranties of fitness for a particular purpose or that this guide is merchantable. Your use of this book indicates your assumption of the risk that it may contain errors and is an acknowledgment of your own sole responsibility for your climbing safety.

Contents

Ivan Greene
makes short
work of
Crystal Ball
Mantle V5R at
Stoney Point.

Overview

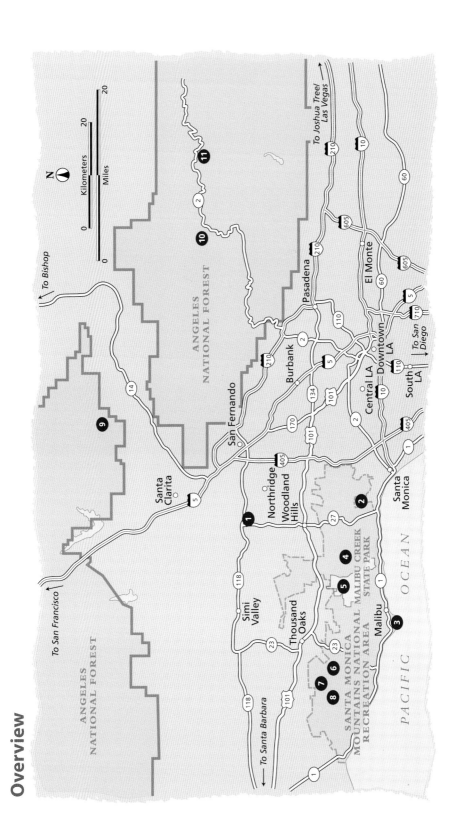

Sunset over downtown LA

Acknowledgments

I'd like to thank the climbers that have come before me and showed the way to escape the clutch of Los Angeles by establishing the amazing routes detailed in this guide. I'd also like to thank the people who have spent large portions of their lives making sure these climbing areas have good access trails and stay clean, safe, and, of course, fun! Climbing in Los Angeles is a passion for many, and I would like to thank the dedicated few who have written detailed guidebooks for the thousands of routes around Los Angeles County. I would also like to thank the climbers who volunteered their time to help make some amazing images for this book. A huge thank-you to all these people: Louie Anderson, Matt Oliphant, Bill Leventhal, Darshan Etz, Jeff Constine, Steve Edwards and Doniel Drazien, Mike Draper, John Mireles, Jack Marshall, John Long, John Yablonski, Troy Mayr, Scott Loomis, Chris Owen, Craig Fry, Jeff Johnson, James March, Tom Gilje, John Bachar, Yvon Chouinard, Royal Robbins, Bob Kamps, Michael Reardon, Nikki Reardon, Crystalyn Falk, Jason Falk, Gary Boisvert, Alvin Hsing, David Meyers, Isamer Bilog, Norman Montes, Tommy Lutz, Stephanie Cronshaw, Victor Ramirez, Shawn Diamond, Natasha Barnes, and Aaron Sandlow—and to everyone else who was, is, and will be a part of the Los Angeles climbing community.

Introduction

Amid the hustle of Los Angeles County, rock climbers can find solitude and beauty tucked into the nooks and crannies of the 4,500-square-mile metropolis. From clipping bolts with humpback whales and dolphins on the edge of the Pacific Ocean, to bouldering at 6,100 feet on pristine alpine granite, to following in the footsteps of Yvon Chouinard, John Bachar, John Long, Royal Robbins, and Michael Reardon, some of the most iconic rock climbing heroes of our generation, Los Angeles truly has it all. Add in the fact that you can actually surf the majestic waves of Malibu, snowboard at Mount Baldy, and still have time for a quick bouldering session at Stoney Point, and you have reason enough to visit LA.

This book will give you all the information necessary to access the natural rock treasures Los Angeles has to offer to outdoor climbing enthusiasts. The rock quality, purity of the lines, and beautiful surroundings will provide experiences you can enjoy and help preserve for generations to come.

How to Use This Guide

The sport routes, topropes, trad climbs, and boulder problems in this book have been selected from the thousands of lines in Los Angeles County based on their rock quality; purity of line (natural lines of weakness up the cliff); fun, interesting, unique, or noteworthy climbing; existing climber access trails; and approaches and descents that do not cause degradation to the fragile environment.

Directions (e.g., "go right" or "climb up and left," etc.) are given as if you are facing the route. Routes are generally listed from left to right as you face the cliff. Directions for climbing down, descending, rappelling, etc., are given for the same orientation (as if you were facing the route from the start of the route). Generally routes are descended by a standard rappel and boulder problems have an obvious descent or walk off, unless otherwise noted.

On most routes, pitch lengths (e.g., 80 feet) are given; these are estimates and not exact figures. Route lines drawn on the photo topos are approximations; every effort has been made to depict the exact line of the route, but as always, trust your own judgment. Dangerous routes have been listed with an "R" rating, and caution is advised when attempting one of these routes.

Difficulty Ratings

The difficulty rating system used in this guidebook for roped routes is the Yosemite Decimal System (YDS), the system used throughout the United States.

A typical Tuesday evening at Stoney Point

Climbing routes are rated on an ascending scale from 5.0 (the easiest climbs requiring ropes and belays) to 5.15 (currently the most difficult climbs). Within the 5.10, 5.11, 5.12, 5.13, 5.14, and 5.15 categories, the subgrades of a, b, c, and d are used to denote finer distinctions in difficulty.

The "V" rating scale, which is used for the boulder problems in this guidebook, has become the standard boulder grading scale in the United States. Boulder problems are rated on an ascending scale from V0 (the easiest problems) to V16 (currently the most difficult boulder problems).

A climb may feel harder for some and easier for others depending on one's height, arm span, leg span, and so on. Over time you should get a feel for the grading scale and be able to make your own decisions; the grades are offered only to give you a general sense of difficulty.

Any climb that is dangerous due to fall potential, length of runouts between bolts, or sheer height has been marked with an "R" next to the rating.

Geology

The geology of Los Angeles mainly comprises the San Gabriel Mountains (Angeles National Forest) and the Santa Monica Mountains. According to the USGS website, the San Gabriel Mountains are a fault-bounded block of ancient crystalline rocks that rises north of the Los Angeles Basin. The eastern end of the mountains rises abruptly to an elevation of over 10,000 feet. To the north the mountains descend more gradually to the Mojave Desert, and to the west to the Sierra Pelona and the Soledad Basin. The range is bounded on the north by the San Andreas Fault zone, on the south and southwest by the Cucamonga–Sierra Madre fault complex, and on the east by faults of the San Jacinto zone. The interior of the range is complexly deformed by faults of many different ages and tectonic styles. A low-angle tectonic dislocation known as the Vincent Thrust created two types of rock in the San Gabriels: the lower plate formed of a complex of metamorphosed sedimentary and volcanic rocks known as the

Michael Reardon satiates his urge to climb on a morning stroll in the heart of LA.

Pelona Schist, and the upper plate rocks that include the very old metamorphic and plutonic rocks (granite).

The Santa Monica Mountains are composed of igneous and sedimentary rocks formed under the sea some 20 million years ago. The range was created by repeated episodes of uplifting and submergence by the Raymond Fault. Topanga and Malibu Creeks have formed gorges that run hundreds of feet deep on their way to the Pacific Ocean. Tilted sandstone beds are a feature in the Santa Monica Mountains at Saddle Peak. On the north slopes west of Malibu Canyon, volcanic rocks have eroded into buttes.

Preparation

To prepare for climbing outdoors on real rock, it is best to familiarize yourself with the sport of rock climbing by joining a rock climbing gym and taking one of their available courses or by taking a rock climbing class or guided trip with an outdoor climbing guiding service (see appendix). Be sure to have all permits needed for the area where you plan to climb (see "Wilderness Permit Requirements" below), and make sure to check the "Equipment and Essentials List" to ensure you have a safe and fun experience.

Climbing Seasons

Climbing is possible year-round in Los Angeles County. Summer may be the least desirable time to climb, even though average temperatures from July to September are only 84 degrees Fahrenheit. In the summer months shade and cooler temps can be found on the Pacific coastline at Point Dume, in the deep and shaded canyon of Malibu Creek State Park, and at the higher elevations of Angeles National Forest. Many locals climb after 4 p.m. during the summer months, as the sun sets well past 8 p.m. Springtime, from March to May, offers climbers a lush and green version of Los Angeles; this is when a majority of its 15 inches of annual rainfall comes, and it makes a world of difference to the array of tropical plant life that grows abundantly here. Los Angeles sees nearly 300 days of sunshine a year, so when autumn and winter roll around, climbing season hits its prime. Temperatures average in the mid-60s, with lows hitting the mid-40s.

A majority of the rock in LA County is volcanic breccia, conglomerate, and sandstone, so caution is advised when climbing after a rainstorm. Locals use the three-day rule to let the porous sandstone dry out completely. Many classic lines have changed their appearance over the years, typically from someone grabbing a little too hard after a rainstorm.

Equipment and Essentials List
- Helmet
- Rope (60 meters/180 feet of 9½ to 11mm diameter)
- Harness
- Carabiners (2 locking D)
- Traditional climbing rack (full set of nuts/stoppers, full set of cams 0.5 inch to 4 inches)
- 8 to 14 quickdraws (depending on the area)
- Webbing/slings/cordage
- Sunglasses
- Water/windproof shell
- First-aid kit
- Sunburn protection (sunblock/hat)
- Flashlight and/or headlamp
- Water
- Snacks/food

Climbing Rack
Most of the climbing in this book can be accomplished with a 60-meter rope and ten to fourteen quickdraws. It will be handy to take along extra slings, webbing, and locking carabiners to some locations for anchors, in particular Stoney Point, where there is an abundance of toproping. A basic traditional rack of gear

A southern sagebrush lizard soaks up the sun in Angeles National Forest.

will suffice for the trad climbing at Horse Flats. A bouldering pad is a nice addition when climbing at Stoney Point and Horse Flats and will help prevent any foot, leg, and ankle injuries.

Land Management and Closures

As of 2014 the following closures were in effect. Climbing is not permitted upstream from the Grotto at Echo Cliffs. Please stay on the routes listed in the book for this area due to the endangered Dudleya succulent growing on the cliffs and near the stream. Climbing on the other large formation at the Lookout is also prohibited due to the possibility of rocks falling onto the road; please stay on the main crag described in this book. There is also a no bolting law in effect at Malibu Creek State Park; locals are working with the park rangers to come up with a solution for bolt replacements.

No-Trace Ethic

You can practice Leave No Trace principles from the moment you step out of your car. Always use the marked trails and climber's paths when available. If there is no marked trail to the cliff, minimize your impact by walking on durable surfaces (i.e., a rock slab or barren ground).

If nature calls and you are far away from any outhouse, deposit solid human waste well away from the base of any climbing site or water source by digging a cathole 8 inches deep. Cover and disguise the cathole when done. Pack out all toilet paper and tampons in a baggie. Urinate on base ground of rock, not plants. Urine contains salt, and animals will dig into plants to get to it.

The Leave No Trace Seven Principles
Plan Ahead and Prepare
Travel and Camp on Durable Surfaces
Dispose of Waste Properly
Leave What You Find
Minimize Campfire Impacts
Respect Wildlife
Be Considerate of Other Visitors

Respect the resident wildlife. Pick up all food crumbs, and don't feed any animals—this habituates them to human food and encourages them to beg and scavenge for food. Keep an eye on your pack at the base of any cliff; squirrels will chew right through it to get food.

For more information on outdoor climbing ethics, visit www.LNT.org or the Access Fund website at www.accessfund.org.

To Report Climbing Accidents
In most areas, to report a climbing accident or other emergency, dial 911. Cell phones are the usual method of reporting accidents and summoning rescues, but they don't work everywhere in the mountains, especially if not fully charged before you get to the climbing destination where cell service is sometimes questionable. If you cannot contact a 911 operator, dial "0" and ask for the emergency dispatch operator or county sheriff. The county sheriff is responsible for coordinating mountain rescue operations in most areas.

Wilderness Permit Requirements
Angeles National Forest requires a National Forest Adventure Pass for day-use parking at Texas Canyon, Horse Flats, and Spring Crag. You can purchase a day pass or a year pass at any of the outdoor gear vendors in Los Angeles and at 7-11s, gas stations, or local markets near the national forest. They can also be found at the ranger station at the junction of Angeles Crest Highway and Angeles Forest Highway or online at www.kinsale.com or www.myscenicdrives.com.

The view from Saddle Peak Road

Texas Canyon

Climb Finder

Best Boulder Problems

Thin Crack, V0, Horse Flats

Three Pigs, V1, Stoney Point

Spiral Traverse, V2, Stoney Point

Bow Sprits, V2, Horse Flats

B1 Face, V2, Horse Flats

Crowd Pleaser (aka Yabo Roof), V2R, Stoney Point

The Yardarm, V3, Horse Flats

Kodas Corner, V3, Stoney Point

Dragon Flake, V5, Horse Flats

Crystal Ball Mantle, V5R, Stoney Point

Best Topropes

Right Edge, 5.5, Stoney Point

Lefthand Route, 5.7, Stoney Point

Beethoven's Crack, 5.7, Stoney Point

Paul's Hole (aka George's Overhang), 5.9, Stoney Point

Christmas Pump, 5.10a, Malibu Creek

747, 5.10c, Stoney Point

West Face Left, 5.10c, Point Dume

Planet of the Apes, 5.11a, Malibu Creek

Maggie's Farm, 5.11b, Stoney Point

Ant Line, 5.11c, Horse Flats

Best Single-Pitch Sport Routes

The Arete, 5.6, Point Dume

Chopping Block, 5.8, Malibu Creek

Agua Negra, 5.9, Texas Canyon

Game Boy, 5.9, Echo Cliffs

Gorgeous, 5.10a, Malibu Creek

Double Agent, 5.10a, The Lookout

Circus Midget, 5.10c, Tick Rock

Loose Nut, 5.10d, Spring Crag

Espresso, 5.11a, Echo Cliffs

The Drifter, 5.12a, Malibu Creek

Stoney Point fills up with blooming Santa Susana Monkey Flowers in the lush springtime.

Map Legend

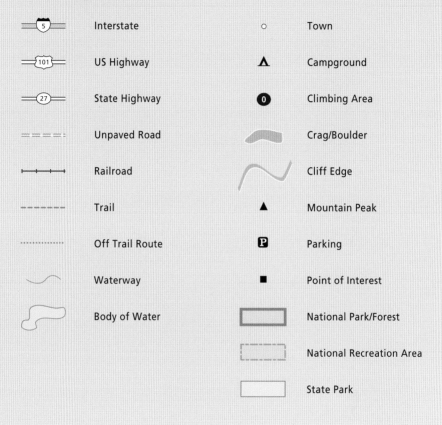

Interstate		Town	
US Highway		Campground	
State Highway		Climbing Area	
Unpaved Road		Crag/Boulder	
Railroad		Cliff Edge	
Trail		Mountain Peak	
Off Trail Route		Parking	
Waterway		Point of Interest	
Body of Water		National Park/Forest	
		National Recreation Area	
		State Park	

Sunset over downtown LA

San Fernando Valley

The San Fernando Valley is home to the first legitimate bouldering area in the country, Stoney Point Park in Chatsworth. The "Valley," as everyone refers to it, sits between the rolling hills and deep canyons of the Santa Monica Mountains to the south and the high-elevation peaks of the Angeles National Forest to the north. Temperatures in the Valley tend to get a little warmer than the rest of the county, so it is best to avoid climbing in the summer months, unless you are out for an evening or early morning session.

If you have a craving for fish when in the area, the Valley is home to "Sushi Row" (aka Ventura Boulevard), known for its noteworthy sushi restaurants. Katsu-ya is always a local favorite, while *Zagat Survey* named Sushi Nozawa (Studio City) and Leila's (Oak Park) among the top five best food picks in Los Angeles.

San Fernando Valley

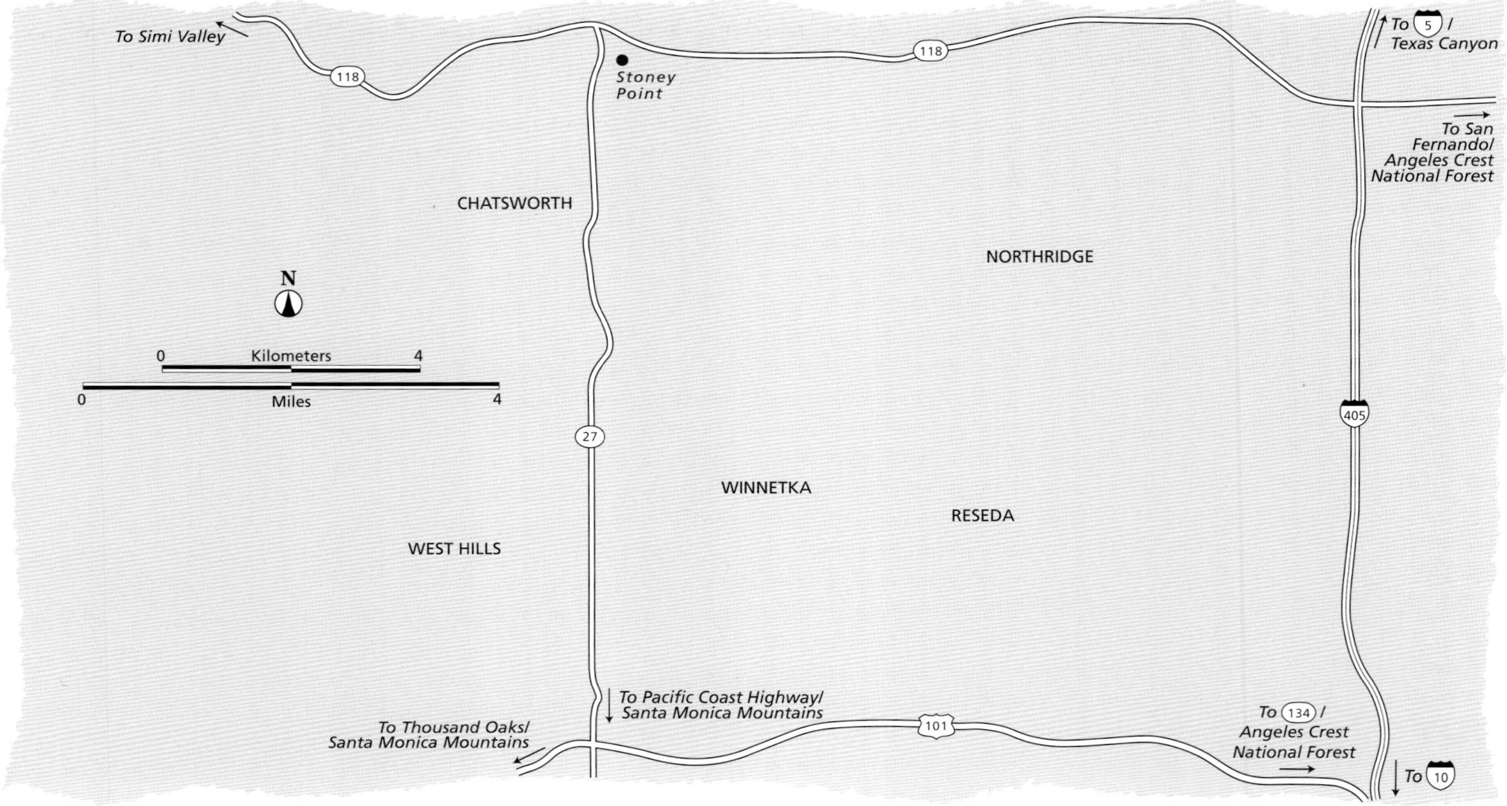

1.

Stoney Point

Stoney Point is Los Angeles's oldest outdoor climbing area and the country's first "bouldering area"; its sandstone walls and boulders have been used by climbers for over eighty years now. Every boulder problem has at least one variation—a common theme among the gym-like boulders of Stoney Point. Locals test each other with harder variations of classic and not so classic lines. It's all part of the amazing experience Stoney Point will surely provide on your visit.

At Stoney Point it is easy to follow in the footsteps of such American rock climbing legends as Royal

Stoney Point

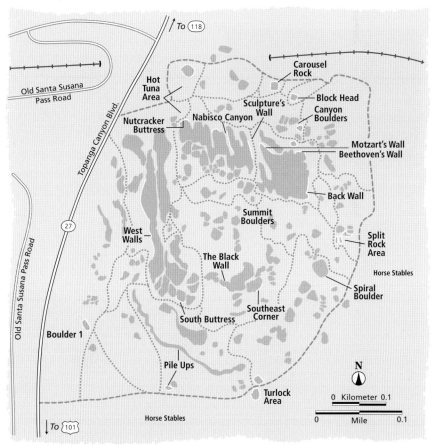

Robbins, Ron Kauk, John Long, Lynn Hill, Yvon Chouinard, John Bachar, Michael Reardon, and Bob Kamps. Some of these luminaries went on to spearhead groundbreaking first ascents of dream climbs such as the Salathé and North America walls on El Capitan or bold free solo ascents in Yosemite and Joshua Tree.

If you plan on taking advantage of the outstanding toproping that Stoney Point has to offer, make sure you bring plenty of slings or webbing, locking carabiners, and a small rack of cams or nuts. Please be aware of the porous sandstone and don't climb at Stoney Point for at least three days after it rains.

> Royal Robbins hopped freight trains as a teen. One day as the train slowed for the turn before a tunnel, he hopped off and discovered a hidden climbing gem called Stoney Point.

Getting there: From the south take US 101 via either the north or south and exit at Topanga Canyon Boulevard (CA 27), then head north. Drive 7 miles and you will see the crag on your right; park according to signage on the east side of the road. From the north take CA 118 from either the east or west and exit at Topanga Canyon Boulevard, then head south. Drive past the traffic light and make a U-turn when possible; park according to the local signs on the east side of the road.

Finding the crag: From the southern end of the crag, a gated dirt road next to the horse pens takes you right to the boulders and main formation. The routes are listed from this entrance heading around the crag in a counterclockwise direction. From the north end of the park, near the streetlight at Santa Susana Pass Road, a dirt footpath leads up the hill to Chouinard's Hole and Hot Tuna.

Boulder 1

BOULDER 1

This is a common place for crowds to gather any day of the week. Tuesday and Thursday evenings are a great time to meet the locals, who have been gathering here at the same time for decades.

Finding the boulder: This is the first boulder you will encounter to your left when entering from the southern entrance.

Descent: Downclimb the slabby east side of the boulder.

Nylon Boy, V1

Just to the left of Boot Flake. Good flakes and dynamic movements lead to a crux final move to the flat-topped mantle.

Boot Flake, V2

The crux is to static or dyno your way to the obvious Boot Flake. Move past the boot, trending slightly to the right for a committing finish up the tall face.

Boulder 1 Traverse, V4

Start on the south side of the boulder on the large ledge and climb in a clockwise direction. There are jugs, crimps, slopers, ledges, and every kind of move in between. Follow the natural path of weakness around the boulder; depending on your height you may wish to stay low or high in certain sections.

Boulder 1

Three Pigs

The Nose

Three Pigs, V1

Part of *Rock & Ice*'s All Time Tick List, this is where some of the original climbers at Stoney practiced their aid climbing techniques before moving on to Yosemite's towering walls. Climb through the three obvious pin scars to a good sloping lip.

The Nose, V0

The obvious arête on the far right side of the east face. Fun lieback moves and a little mantle to start the arête lead to great jugs and an airy slab.

SOUTH BUTTRESS AREA

The toprope routes here feature roofs and slabs that can easily be anchored by slinging a boulder at the summit and backing it up with cams or nuts. To access the top, walk to the right of the wall and follow a trail around the

corner and up to the left past some slabs. The wall is about 45 feet tall.

Finding the crag: These are the buttresses on the south side of Stoney Point that are easily seen from Boulder 1. To approach, from the north side of Boulder 1, walk straight up the climber's path and gradually to the right toward the series of buttresses.

Eye of Faith, 5.10c

Navigate your way through the roof and pull the lip to establish yourself on the headwall. Climb up toward the Eye for a rest before you race the pump to the top.

Paul's Hole (aka George's Overhang), 5.9

One of the better moderates in the park. Climb up to the small overhang, don't crawl into the hole and get

South Buttress Area

Eye of Faith

Paul's Hole

stuck in an awkward position. Continue past the hole with some high-stepping and stemming to access the easy upper slab.

THE BLACK WALL

This freestanding wall provides a great 5.11 that gets sun all morning and afternoon.

Finding the crag: From the previous routes, head to the right along the buttresses. You will come to an open area in a gully; continue across

this toward a face that has BOB spray painted near the top just below a tree. The route is about 40 feet tall and can be anchored by slinging a tree and backing it up with nuts and/or cams.

The Black Wall (aka Nose Cone), 5.11a
This route starts to the right of the graffiti DX and climbs the dark streak of wall that is full of long pulls on great pockets, edges, and flakes.

The Black Wall

The Black Wall

PILE UPS

The boulder closest to the trail contains the short and powerful classics, and tops out around 8 to 10 feet.

Finding the boulder: From Boulder 1 walk east along the dirt path (you will walk along a horse stable on your right). After a minute you will encounter the Pile Ups area on your left.

Descent: Walk off the left slab of the boulder.

Pile Driver, V3

The direct line on the left side. Start low on a large hold and move through a couple of crimps to gain the lip, then mantle.

Pile Lieback, V2

Stand-start in the center of the boulder on some polished holds to gain a sidepull for your left hand. Make a big move to the ledge and top out.

Gomer Pile V4

The sit-start to Pile Lieback, this route adds a couple of excellent hard moves.

Todd's Traverse (aka The Amphitheatre), V0

Todd's Traverse can be seen directly up the hill on a short cliff band and is an excellent 20-foot traverse through a series of pockets, cracks, and bulges. Start on the right side and climb to the left following the largest holds on the wall, past a vertical crack to an easier finish.

Pile Ups

TURLOCK AREA

This is a great place to hone your highball skills, and there are endless problems and variations between the two main boulders. John Yablonski made the Turlock Boulder famous with his addition of Yabo Roof (aka Crowd Pleaser) in the 1970s.

Finding the boulders: From the Pile Ups continue east down the main dirt path for another minute. You will walk straight to Turlock Boulder; B1 Boulder is just to the left.

Descent: An easy downclimb that resembles a staircase is to the right of The Flake on the Turlock Boulder. To descend from the B1 Boulder, scramble down the backside through a tree.

Turlock Boulder

The Flake, V0

The obvious flake system running from left to right on the west face of Turlock Boulder. Good sloping edges and undercling the flake lead you to a committing final move at the lip.

Crystal Ball Mantle, V5R

A mega classic. Jump-start to the big crystal ball under the overhang. Maneuver your right foot up next to the ball and use a small sidepull for the right hand to stand up and make a huge move with the left hand to a flake. Match the flake, make a move to a good left hand, and fire to the right-hand jug. Commit to the heel hook and mantle.

Turlock Boulder

Crowd Pleaser (aka Yabo Roof), V2R

A highball classic, put up by stone-master John Yablonski. Climb the arête for a couple of moves and then move right to the flakes under the overhang. Make some excellent gymnastic moves to the lip and commit to the rock over to the upper face.

B1 Boulder

Masters of Reality, V5/6

This climb has changed over the years due to the upper holds reforming anytime someone climbs on it too soon after a rainstorm—thus the split grade. Opposing pressure leads to a thumb undercling, high-stepping and some stemming before you make the move to the dish. Match the dish and use some precise footwork to the final bad slopers at the top.

Expansion Chamber, V7

Sit start with burly open-handed slopers and bad feet to work your way up the arête to some decent edges. Use delicate footwork for the topout.

The Ear, V3

This is the Bob Kamps's area testpiece. Stand-start with your hands in the bottom of the "Ear." Climb up into the "Ear" using gastons and sidepulls. Once standing, use delicate slopers to the top. Sit-start for a V6 variation.

B1 Boulder

Apsema, V6

On the boulder's south face, start on the two-finger stacked pocket at face height. Power up left to the rail by either jumping off the ground or using a bad left-hand hold. Finish directly up using sidepulls and slopers.

The Crack, V3

A rite of passage for V3 climbers, this is the obvious disjointed crack on the right of the face. Stand-start for the V3 variation or sit down to make it a V5. Climb the polished crack with powerful moves to the upper slopers at the lip.

SOUTHEAST CORNER

Old pin scars from days past have created a fun manufactured wall. Scramble up the left side to access the top of this 35-foot wall. Use cams in the cracks near the lip or sling a boulder and use gear for backup.

Finding the crag: Approach the Southeast Corner from the Turlock Boulder by heading directly uphill toward the main crag. Trend to your right to locate the obvious Pin Scars wall.

Pin Scars (aka Machine Gun), 5.9

The right-hand line of pin scars. It is possible to lead this route by using small cams. Follow the pin scars up and to the right until they peter out; finish up on a slab.

Southeast Corner

Pin Scars

Spiral Boulder

Spiral Traverse

SPIRAL BOULDER

This boulder has a handful of excellent moderates, including the awesome Spiral Traverse. The boulder gets a lot of morning and late afternoon shade.

Finding the boulder: From the Turlock Area, continue down the dirt footpath. After a minute you will walk between two boulders on the trail; look for a climber's trail up the hill to the left. The Spiral Boulder is on your left.

Descent: Downclimb the slab on the right side.

Spiral Traverse, V2

A great traverse that starts way down and left on huge flakes and jugs. Work your way up and right into the thin middle section. Continue climbing to the large rail at the far right side; top out here.

Yvon Chouinard, owner of Patagonia Clothing, came to Stoney Point when he was practicing falconry and learning how to rappel into falcon nests. This is where he first saw rock climbers and discovered his new passion.

Split Rock Area

Johnson Problem

Powerglide

SPLIT ROCK AREA

This area contains some excellent hard testpieces. Powerglide is at the top of everyone's list.

Finding the boulders: From the Spiral Boulder, return to and continue down the main dirt path; soon you will see an open gully on the left with Powerglide and Johnson Problem facing you. These two climbs get morning and early afternoon sun, while the boulders on the back stay in the shade most of the day.

Descent: Scramble down the left side of Powerglide. For the other climbs, scramble off the back near Vaino Problem.

Johnson Problem, V8R

A large roof with a tufa-like feature leads to a good jug then long moves to bad sloping holds at the lip. Bump out to the left arête and work your way up to the tall slab.

Powerglide, V7

An all-time classic. Start under the roof on a large polished sidepull. Move to the slopers on the lip and work your way to the left-hand crimp. Make a big move to the pocket, then top out directly above on slopers.

Split Rock Area

Vaino Problem

Johnson Arete

Vaino Problem, V5

Start with your right hand on the arête and move up to slopers using heel hooks, then crown a couple more slopers to gain the easy topout.

Johnson Arete, V6

Start low with your left hand on the arête and your right in the pocket. Use heel and toe hooks to move up the arête and get a right-hand crimp and then a sidepull. Delicately work your way up the slab to top out.

Back Wall

BACK WALL

A great wall to warm up on before heading into the canyons for some of the harder toprope routes.

Finding the crag: From the backside of Split Rock, follow a small footpath through the brush; you will immediately see the long Back Wall on your left. The following routes are on the left side of the wall. There are many other great toprope routes here to the right. Access the top by scrambling up the left side of the wall or by going through the canyon near Beethoven's Wall. Sling boulders or use nuts and cams for anchors. About 35 feet tall.

Potholes, 5.9

A great line up the huge holes on the left side of the wall. The top is the crux.

Potholes Traverse, V1

Traverse from the crack to the right of Potholes for 20 feet to the right. Many variations exist.

Block Head

Yabo Arete

BLOCK HEAD

The aesthetic Yabo Arete is the stand-out highball in the backside of Stoney Point. This line requires pads and spotters due to the uneven landing.

Finding the boulder: Continue on the main trail past the Split Rock area for a couple of minutes, then make a left-hand turn around to the backside of the park. You will soon arrive at the solitary Block Head boulder on your left near the train tunnel.

Descent: Downclimb at the lowest point on the arête to the left of Yabo Arete.

Yabo Arete, V8R

Climb the striking arête on the north side of the boulder. Start with a left-hand pocket and bad right hand. High-step and make a huge move to better holds. Move up and left to a pocket and a solid mantle at the top.

> Highlining has become a popular sport at Stoney Point over the last decade. In 2004 Aron Stockhausen was the first to walk the now classic Aron's Gap, a 32-foot line, 40 feet above Nabisco Canyon.

Local Aaron Sandlow takes another
lap on the imposing Yabo Arete.

CAROUSEL ROCK

A large boulder with quite a few problems on it next to the train tunnel.

Finding the boulder: Continue past Block Head on the main trail to the next boulder on your left.

Descent: Downclimbing the tree and rock together on the west side is the easiest descent.

Southwest Corner, V0

The obvious corner with good edges and slopers.

Roller Coaster, V2R

A fun climb on the north face. Climb the face to the pocket and then traverse left to a small ledge. Climb directly up from here on the thin face.

Carousel Rock

Carousel Rock

Night Train, V8R

One of Michael Reardon's final additions to the park. Climb just to the right of Roller Coaster through the undercling roof. Use a series of nonexistent holds, small edges, and divots to work your way to the highest point on the boulder.

BEETHOVEN'S WALL AREA

This is a very popular wall for climbers of all grades. The standouts are the two listed below.

Finding the crag: From the Back Wall continue walking along the cliff until you wrap around a corner to the left; Beethoven's Wall is on the left. To access the top, scramble up the gully to the right. You can sling boulders and use medium to large gear for an anchor; bring extra webbing.

The Prow, 5.11a

One of Michael Reardon's favorites for his solo circuit. Start anywhere on the arête and climb up to a small

Beethoven's Wall Area

Beethoven's Crack

The Prow

Scrambled Eggs Traverse

ledge. Follow the arête and just to the right of it on small sloping edges and crimps to the top.

Beethoven's Crack, 5.7

Climb the left-leaning crack to start, then head directly up to a ledge. Traverse to the right to finish up another crack system.

Scrambled Eggs Traverse, V4

This boulder is just in front and to the right of Beethoven's Wall. Start on the far right side of the boulder and climb to a ledge, then traverse to the left. As the ledge worsens, make a big move to a hole out left. Top out up and left from here.

CANYON BOULDERS

This small cluster of boulders contains some real gems and will offer some seclusion from the crowds on a busy day.

Finding the boulders: From Beethoven's Wall head toward the Scrambled Eggs Traverse and turn right down through a corridor. Critter Crack will be on your left before you exit the corridor. Once you exit, look for The Font, the elephant-skinned bulge on the left. If you continue straight after exiting the corridor, you can follow a small path that turns to the left through the brush to Kodas Corner.

Critter Crack, V0

Use finger jams and liebacks on the crack to make your way to a committing finish.

Canyon Boulders

Canyon Boulders

The Font, V7

A Stoney Point testpiece in all its sloping glory. Start on opposing holds under the small overhang, then use terrible feet to gain the sloping dish over the lip. High-step and get ready to fight friction to the top.

Kodas Corner, V3

One of the best of the grade. Use the amazing left arête and good right-hand holds to get high enough to make the long right-hand move to the lip. Mantle out.

Canyon Boulders

Right Edge

Center Route

Lefthand Route

Motzart's Traverse

MOTZART'S WALL

This is a great wall to get a lot of climbing in a short amount of time due to the multiple bolted anchors at the top. The top can be accessed by scrambling up the canyon around the right side of the wall.

Finding the crag: From Beethoven's Wall walk along the base of the cliff; you will quickly come up on Motzart's Wall on your left behind the large boulder and tree.

Motzart's Traverse, V0

The traverse has a fairly flat landing the entire way and is great for getting a burn on. Traverse from left to right; turning the corner at the end is the crux.

Lefthand Route, 5.7

Start under the large pockets, then trend left while climbing excellent edges and flakes. The crux is getting over the overhang at the top of the route.

Center Route, 5.9

Use the same anchors as Lefthand Route. Start to the left of the tree, then make technical moves up the face to the crux 10 feet off the ground. Climb straight up on good holds to the overhang. Traverse to the left to finish.

Right Edge, 5.5

A great beginner's route to help hone in the footwork. Climb up the slabby right arête to the upper crux where there are a couple of tricky moves.

Quickstep, V2

This boulder sits right at the base of Motzart's. Use a large sidepull rail on the left and pin scars on the right to work your way up the arête. Top out on slopers. Climb down to the right and into the tree to descend.

Motzart's Wall

Quickstep

Sculpture's Wall

Sculpture's Crack

Sculpture's Traverse

SCULPTURE'S WALL

The classic of the area features a series of old pin scars that created a gem. Extend the pump by adding on the full traverse before you begin climbing the crack. Access the top by scrambling up the canyon. There are bolts for anchors and cracks for backup gear.

Finding the crag: From Motzart's Wall head past Right Edge and follow a path to the opposite side of the canyon to the obvious pin-scarred wall.

Sculpture's Crack, 5.10c

Climb up the leftmost crack system with lots of liebacking on old pin scars. Fight the pump and climb into the slot on the right to top out.

Sculpture's Traverse, V2

Start on the right with a tough lieback move to the large ledge. Traverse across and get a rest at the base of Sculpture's Crack before heading into the final bulge around the corner. Finish at an obvious jug.

NABISCO CANYON

This is a great canyon to climb in on a hot afternoon; it gets very little sunlight and stays cool even on the hottest days. There are many great moderates on the east wall and lots of pumpy overhangs on the west wall. Access the top by scrambling up the canyon. There are bolts for anchors.

Finding the crag: From Sculpture's Wall head out of the canyon and follow the path to the left and around the corner. Nabisco Canyon is on your left.

Maggie's Farm, 5.11b

This line starts in the wide crack on the right side of the west wall. Follow the crack up and to the right using some hidden holds. Once you leave the crack, climb through a series of pin scars that lead back left to the anchors.

Nabisco Canyon

Maggie's Farm

Nabisco Canyon

Maggie's Traverse

Maggie's Traverse, V2

A fantastic traverse that sits in the shade and offers over 80 feet of climbing. Climb from the far left side of the east wall and head right. The first crux comes early with a big move to a ledge and some tricky moves once you pass the tree. After this you start to climb up, gaining good holds and ledges. The other crux comes at the end when you make technical moves to the final wide crack where you can exit.

NUTCRACKER BUTTRESS

This wall contains some great moderates on the same anchor. Routes are about 40 feet. Access the top by scrambling up the canyon to the right of the routes. There are bolts on top that can be backed up with slings and gear.

Finding the crag: From Nabisco Canyon follow the footpath out of the canyon and around to the left; the next large buttress on your left is Nutcracker Buttress.

Nutcracker, 5.10a

Climb up a slab and into an alcove to a horizontal break where you make tricky moves out right to the bulge. Head up from here to the pin scars near the top.

747, 5.10c

This route starts around the corner of the buttress on the right side. Use some large holds to pass the first bulge, then move up to the second crux bulge and climb the slab to the top.

Nutcracker Buttress

Nutcracker

747

Stephanie Cronshaw gets some extra endurance laps on Hot Tuna (V5) at Stoney Point.

HOT TUNA AREA

This is a great spot to escape the heat. Locals kids like to hang out and party here, and you'll see the aftereffects; please pick up what you can.

Finding the boulders: Continue on the trail from Nutcracker Buttress, heading out to an open patch of the park. Walk toward Topanga Canyon Boulevard; Hot Tuna is up the hill to your left under the huge overhang. From the northern parking area on Topanga Canyon Boulevard, this is the first roof you'll see on your right as you head up the dirt path from the traffic light.

Hot Tuna Area

Hot Tuna, V5

This area classic is a long overhanging roof traverse with fun moves on polished holds. Start on the far left side of the cave and head right. Finish with a big move to a sloping hold just outside the roof.

Mickey Mouse, V5R

This highball starts on good holds at the bottom of a crack. Make a long move up and into the crack, then head left to the bulge. Traverse around the left for a couple of moves, then top out on the slab.

The stonemasters left their mark on Stoney Point, too. John Bachar opened up Ummagumma, V7, John Yablonski did the first ascent of Yabo Arete, V8, and John Long gave us Largonot, V6.

Hot Tuna Area

Chouinard's Hole

Chouinard's Hole, V2

A party trick climb established by
the great Yvon Chouinard. This climb
is on the huge boulder right next to
the highway, across the path from
the Hot Tuna cave. Climb into the
hole and sit down!

WEST WALLS

These walls have nice long (up to
80 feet) routes and get shade in the
morning. Access the top by soloing up
S-Crack or by scrambling up the buttress to the right of the wall. Bring nuts,
cams, and long slings for the anchors.

Finding the crag: It is easiest to
access West Walls from Boulder 1. Follow the footpath directly behind Boulder 1 up toward the main crag. Stay to
the left of the walls; you will arrive at
the West Wall on your right after a few
minutes of hiking uphill. You can also
access the crag by following a faint
path uphill from Topanga Canyon
Boulevard, about 100 yards south of
the traffic light.

West Walls

S-Crack, 5.4

This mellow crack is often soloed by locals and is a good route for beginners to practice wide cracks on easy terrain.

Ozymandias, 5.11b

Start underneath the large hueco and climb up to the ledge. Traverse to the right past a groove to steeper terrain. Climb directly up from here into the black face, heading to the right at the top.

Jesus Wall Left, 5.10c

Start to the right of the large chimney that splits the main wall. Climb up to the large ledge, then traverse to the right and head up the depression. When the depression ends, traverse to the left and finish up the arête.

Central Route, 5.11a

Start just left of an old bolt ladder. Mantle to the ledge and climb left to a crack; follow the crack to a horizontal crack. From here climb to the right and establish on the face, then finish up and right on face holds.

SUMMIT BOULDERS

One of the ultimate classics at Stoney Point, Ummagumma was put up by John Bachar in the 1970s. Come climb on some history.

Finding the boulders: The easiest and most direct way to find the boulders is to hike up the canyon between Motzart's Wall and Sculpture's Crack. Once you get to the top, you'll see the Ummagumma boulder in the clearing about 100 yards in front of you. Or approach by hiking uphill from the Turlock area, following the path up and around toward the summit.

Descent: Scramble down the back off the left side of the boulder.

Ummagumma, V7

Jump-start to the large hueco and make a huge move up and left to a smaller pocket. Exit left or right on a tricky slab.

Fighting with Alligators, V10 (no topo)

A new-school classic. Just around the right corner from Ummagumma. Sit-start in a cave on the left side with an undercling, then climb out right to slopers on the lip. Keep traversing right to finish at a natural exit.

Summit Boulders

Ummagumma

Pacific Coastline and Santa Monica Mountains East

The Pacific coastline and Santa Monica Mountains are one of the major draws of Los Angeles County. Some of the most amazing sunsets, seafood, secluded trails, and breathtaking views can be found here. Point Dume offers beginner-friendly toprope and sport climbing, and it is stacked with stunning views from the volcanic cliff right on the Pacific Ocean. Tick Rock is a secluded sandstone crag tucked just a few miles into the Pacific Palisades that offers high-quality and technical sport climbing.

Malibu is home to some of the best longboarding waves in Southern California. When surfing exploded in the 1950s, Malibu was at its epicenter, boasting innovative surfboard design and some of the biggest names in the sport. It's no wonder every campy surf film wanted to use Malibu's "Perfect Break" in the 1950s and 1960s. Legends like Miki Dora, Kathy Kohner (aka Gidget), and Mickey Munoz called Malibu their home during this time.

The Santa Monica Mountains offer easy access from the north and south and an opportunity to experience a whole other world of seclusion in Los Angeles. The mountains were once home to the Chumash and Tongva Native American tribes, and hundreds of archaeological sites exist here. Some of the more notable finds have been the intricate handwoven baskets that are now on display in the Smithsonian Museum in Washington, DC, and locally at the Museum of Natural History in Santa Barbara. The Santa Monica Mountains are full of great hiking opportunities, including the Backbone Trail that traverses 68 miles across the mountains. Keep an eye out for falcons, hawks, bobcats, mountain lions, ticks, and rattlesnakes—all of which can be found in this area.

The small satellite areas—The Lookout, Backcountry Crags, and Saddle Peak—offer peace and quiet; each location provides a unique rock climbing experience. The views continuously get better as you travel though these stretches of the mountains, usually with the Pacific Ocean just off in the distance. Echo Cliffs and Malibu Creek State Park can be busy on weekends and holidays, but some of the best sport climbing in Southern California can be found on their cliffs.

Pacific Coastline and Santa Monica Mountains East

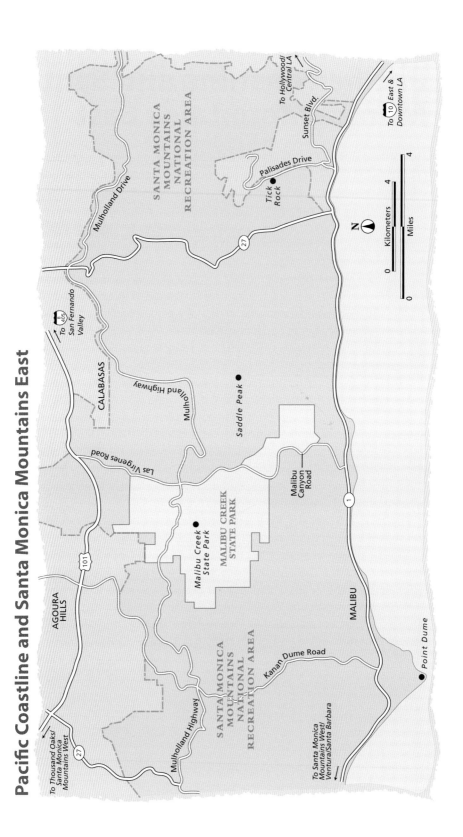

2.

Tick Rock

Tick Rock is a small crag just off the road in the upscale neighborhood of Pacific Palisades. The thickness of the woods surrounding the crag creates a feeling of seclusion. The rock is a very compact gray sandstone and climbs like granite. The routes are high quality and follow a series of discontinuous cracks and technical slabs up the face. The highest point of the crag is about 80 feet. There is some fun bouldering at the base of the crag to warm up on.

Some of the climbers responsible for this little haven include Jeff Constine, Steve Edwards, Darshan Etz, and Doniel Drazien. Jeff in particular has spent a lot of time and effort constructing the trails and belay patios beneath each group of routes. The routes are safely bolted, and there is an excellent bench system at the base of the crag for the peanut gallery.

Some local seafood favorites are Reel Inn, just 3.5 miles away from the crag heading north on the Pacific Coast Highway, and Duke's Malibu, which is another 3.2 miles. Make sure to ask for the catch of the day for some real fresh seafood! If you have extra time in the area, be sure to stop by the Getty Center Museum. Admission is free. Designed by Richard Meier, the architecture of the museum alone is reason to visit. There is also an extensive garden along with the numerous collections of art on permanent display as well as rotating exhibits. The museum is about 10 miles to the east off I-405. For more information visit www.getty.edu.

Getting there: Follow the Pacific Coast Highway (PCH)/CA 1 either north or south and turn onto Sunset Boulevard. Drive 0.5 mile and take a left onto Palisades Drive. Follow this for 1.5 miles to a dirt pullout for parking on the left-hand side of the road under a large tree. Please make sure to make the legal U-turn just up the road; there have been multiple accidents in this spot.

From the east take I-10 west to the PCH, then follow the PCH for 4 miles and take a right onto Sunset Boulevard. Follow the directions above to arrive at the parking.

Finding the crag: The climber's trail and the top of the cliff are visible at the pullout. 1-minute approach.

Tick Rock

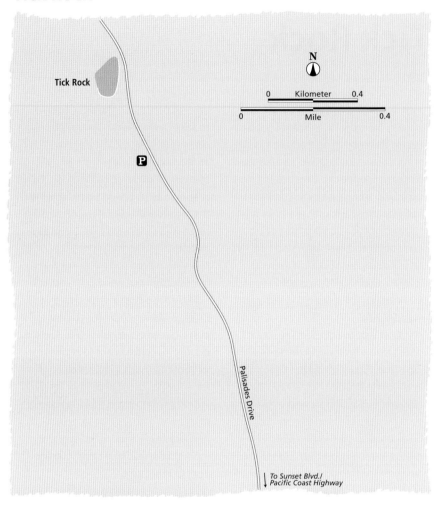

Tick Rock

N

0   Kilometer   0.4

0   Mile   0.4

P

Palisades Drive

To Sunset Blvd./
Pacific Coast Highway

Perro De La Guerra, 5.12c
This is the left line of bolts on the main wall and shares the start with Flying Guillotine. After climbing the right-leaning ramp and clipping two bolts, head slightly left following a corner for the next two bolts. Use some delicate footwork to climb up and left and clip the final three bolts to the top. 7 bolts to anchors. Yahoo Predator, a hard 5.13, is to the left after clipping the second bolt. Many variations of the start exist. (Topo, page 55)

Native Jeff Constine about to wage war with the crux of Perro De La Guerra (5.12c) at Tick Rock

Michael Reardon can be seen cursing at himself during the first free solo attempt of Perro De La Guerra in the Sender Films movie *Return to Sender*. Michael backed off the delicate upper face move three times and downclimbed before everything felt perfect and he made the lieback move on a nothing smear for his left foot. A heart-pounding sequence to watch.

Flying Guillotine, 5.10c

This line shares the same start as Perro De La Guerra, but after the first two bolts, continue up the slab in the middle. Clip the next two bolts and follow the final three bolts to a right-leaning undercling with an optional ½-inch cam placement. 7 bolts to open shuts.

Holy Crap, 5.10a

Start just to the right of Flying Guillotine. Climb the slab and seams to a short roof. Head left to clip the third bolt and join Guillotine to the top. Many variations exist. 7 bolts to open shuts.

Circus Midget, 5.10c

The next set of bolts to the right of Holy Crap. Climb up the middle of the face to a finger lock in the crack directly under a small roof. Pull the roof and finish up the face and arête above. 10 bolts to 2 chains.

Perro Del Amore, 5.12a

This short but fun route starts at the white streak on the right side of the wall just up the climber's trail. Climb through some overlapping holds to the crux on the final slab. 4 bolts to closed shuts.

Turning Point, 5.11d

This climb has the same start as Perro Del Amore, but after clipping the first bolt, start climbing to the right over a steep corner. Follow four more bolts up a faint water streak while climbing good edges to the top. 5 bolts to closed shuts.

Axis of Evil, 5.11a (no topo)

Around the left side of the crag, following a climber's trail, are a few more climbs. The farthest one up the trail—Axis of Evil—has a great belay terrace. Climb straight up the bolts on long moves; the crux traverse comes after the last bolt to the anchors. 6 bolts to chains.

Tick Rock

Norman Montes gets a heavy dose of nature at its finest on West Face Right at the cliff of Point Dume (5.10b).

3.

Point Dume

Point Dume juts out from the Malibu coastline and offers excellent toprope and lead-protected climbing for beginners and intermediates in a stunning setting mere feet from the Pacific Ocean. From December to March it is not uncommon to find yourself 40 feet up the cliff with migrating herds of humpback whales and pods of dolphins cruising by below. The cliff is composed of volcanic rock and features excellent slab climbing options as well as some vertical to overhanging routes on the ocean side. Most of the routes are about 80 feet long.

Getting there: From Los Angeles drive north on the Pacific Coast Highway (PCH) CA 1 toward Malibu. One mile past Kanan Dume Road, turn left onto Westward Beach Road and drive 1.2 miles to the Point Dume parking

Point Dume

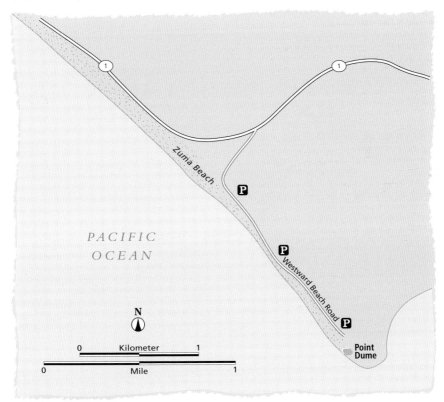

area (fee varies depending on the season). You can park for free on Westward Beach Road, but it's not an easy task in the busy summer months and is a much longer walk to the cliff.

Finding the crag: The crag is visible from the parking area.

Descent: Rappel or walk off along the bluff and down the trail on the left side of the crag. Access the top by hiking the same trail to the left of the crag.

Center Route, 5.8

This climb is in the center of the north face on the beach. Climb up through the depression in the wall on thin edges. Four bolts to bolt anchors over the summit, or anchors to the left on

the face before the summit. Bring long slings for the anchor.

Right Center, 5.7

The bolt line just to the right of Center Route. Climb up to the right of the depression, following four bolts to the same anchors as Center Route.

The Arete, 5.6

The obvious arête on the right corner of the north face. This is an enjoyable route due to the ocean exposure and the ease of climbing up the low-angle arête with small edges; the route stays mostly on the face just left of the arête. Keep your eyes out for whales and dolphins. 5 bolts to bolt anchors.

Point Dume

West Face Left, 5.10c

This is the first route on the ocean side of the crag. It can only be toproped (three-bolt anchor at the top). Start at the base of the huge boulder; begin by climbing flakes and heading up to the right to get over a bulge. Climb up the face to the roof and exit to the left or right.

The buried Statue of Liberty scene in the original *Planet of the Apes* movie was filmed right in front of the cliff at Point Dume.

West Face Right, 5.10b

The bolt line on the right side of the wall. Start up some large jugs and onto the main face, then continue toward the flakes and make some long moves to the pumpy finish. 6 bolts to bolt anchor; bring slings.

Tony Stark's mansion in the *Iron Man* series was digitally placed on top of the cliff line at Point Dume overlooking the Pacific Ocean.

Saddle Peak

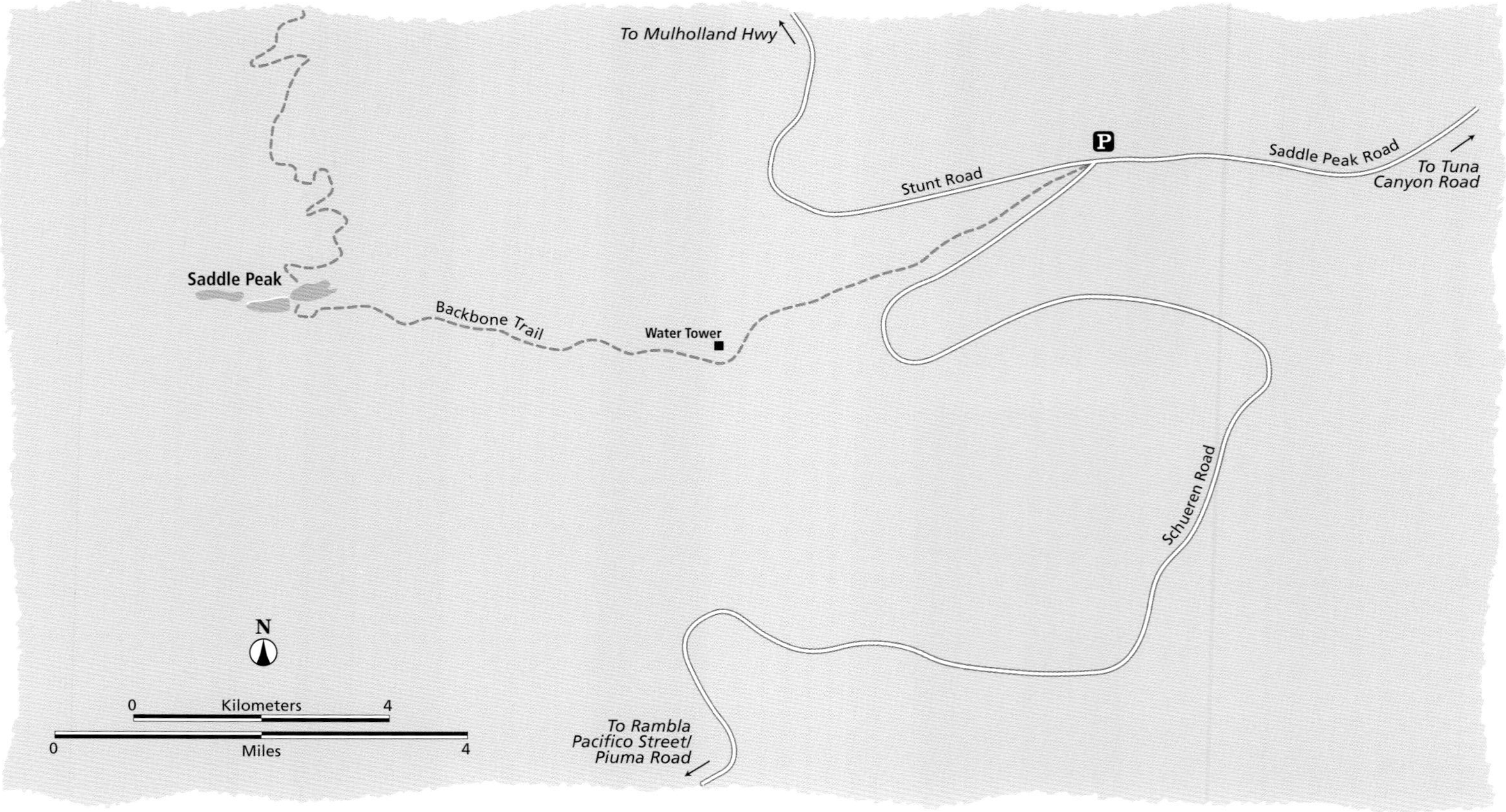

To Tuna Canyon Road

Saddle Peak Road

Schueren Road

Stunt Road

To Mulholland Hwy

Water Tower

Backbone Trail

Saddle Peak

To Rambla Pacifico Street/ Piuma Road

N

Kilometers

Miles

0   4

0   4

Saddle Peak (aka Corpse Wall)

A short drive away from Malibu Creek State Park is Saddle Peak, a great beginner's spot due to its short access hike, easy toprope setup, and numerous 5.9 and under routes. The sandstone crag was developed around 2004. Although the routes seem runout at times, it is only because all the routes can be easily toproped and there are many cracks for optional gear. The crag gets shade for most of the morning and early afternoon.

Getting there: From the north take US 101, exit 29, onto Mulholland Drive/Valley Circle Boulevard and head south. Drive 0.7 mile and take a right onto Valmar Road. Follow Valmar for 1.1 miles to the Mulholland Highway; take a right here. Drive 3.8 miles and turn left onto Stunt Road. Continue on Stunt for 4 miles to a stop sign at a three-way intersection with Schueren Road, Stunt Road, and Saddle Peak Road. Park in the big dirt parking area on the left-hand side.

From the west take the Pacific Coast Highway (PCH)/CA 1 for 15.8 miles east of Decker Canyon Road (CA 23) and turn left onto Las Flores Canyon Road, opposite Duke's Seafood.

Drive 3.4 miles to a T junction at Rambla Pacifico Street/Piuma Road. Take a right here and drive 0.6 mile to Schueren Road. Take another right and follow this road for 1.8 miles to the three-way intersection and parking area.

From the junction of the PCH and I-10, drive 8.9 miles northwest and take a right onto Las Flores Canyon Road, opposite from Duke's Seafood. Follow the directions above from this point.

Finding the crag: From the parking area head west to the little ridge between Stunt Road and Schueren Road and follow the dirt trail toward and past a large water tower. After about 0.5 mile of walking uphill, you will come to a fork in the trail with a No Biking sign; take the smaller footpath that continues straight and down the hill. After a total of about 0.75 mile, you will see the crag on your left. You can access the top easily by walking around the far right side.

The Roof, 5.10a
The first bolted line to the right of the R.I.P. cross at the base of the wall. Start

Ben Hirschfeld climbs into the sunlight on The Roof (5.10a) at Saddle Peak.

by climbing up to a small bush next to the roof and clip the first bolt. The route weaves up the wall with the top being the crux. 7 bolts with a 2-bolt anchor; bring slings.

Xeno Dance, 5.9

The second line of bolts just to the right of the huge break in the cliff. Start climbing up the left or right crack on a block in the wall. Follow faint seams until you must traverse to your left for 8 feet on small xenolith pebbles. Head straight up after the traverse. 7 bolts to 2 chain anchors.

Route 4, 5.9

This route starts about 8 feet to the right of Xeno Dance. Climb up the balancy seam that leans to the right and establish on the face. Climb with

a crack to your right most of the way, past a small bush on your right and then straight up to the anchors. 6 bolts to chain anchors.

Route 5, 5.8

The next set of bolts to the right of Route 4. Start up a crack and climb through slabs and disjointed seams, passing the small bush on your left. The crux comes at the face just below the anchors. 7 bolts to chain anchors.

Route 6, 5.8

This is a great variation to Route 5. Start just below the tree that is growing out of the crack above. Climb up using the varying cracks on the right. After the third bolt the route merges into Route 5. 7 bolts to chain anchors.

Saddle Peak (aka Corpse Wall)

Christmas Chronicle, 5.10a

Continue down the wall to a vertical white streak. Just past the white streak is a bush growing out of the wall; this climb starts just left of the bush. Make some tricky moves at the start to gain the balancy upper slab. 4 bolts to chain anchors.

Last Dance, 5.10d

Currently the last and hardest route on the wall. Start just to the right of the small bush in the wall. Climb up to the roof where you can clip the first bolt and make the long crux move. Establish on the upper slab and enjoy easier climbing to the top past a good ledge. 5 bolts to a chain anchor.

A young man's body was found just down the hill from the base of the crag by some of the crag's pioneers. It was said that a suicide note was found near the body, so the arête on the far left side of the wall is called R.I.P. Arete (not described in this guidebook) and a cross was installed at the base of the route in his memory.

Malibu Creek State Park

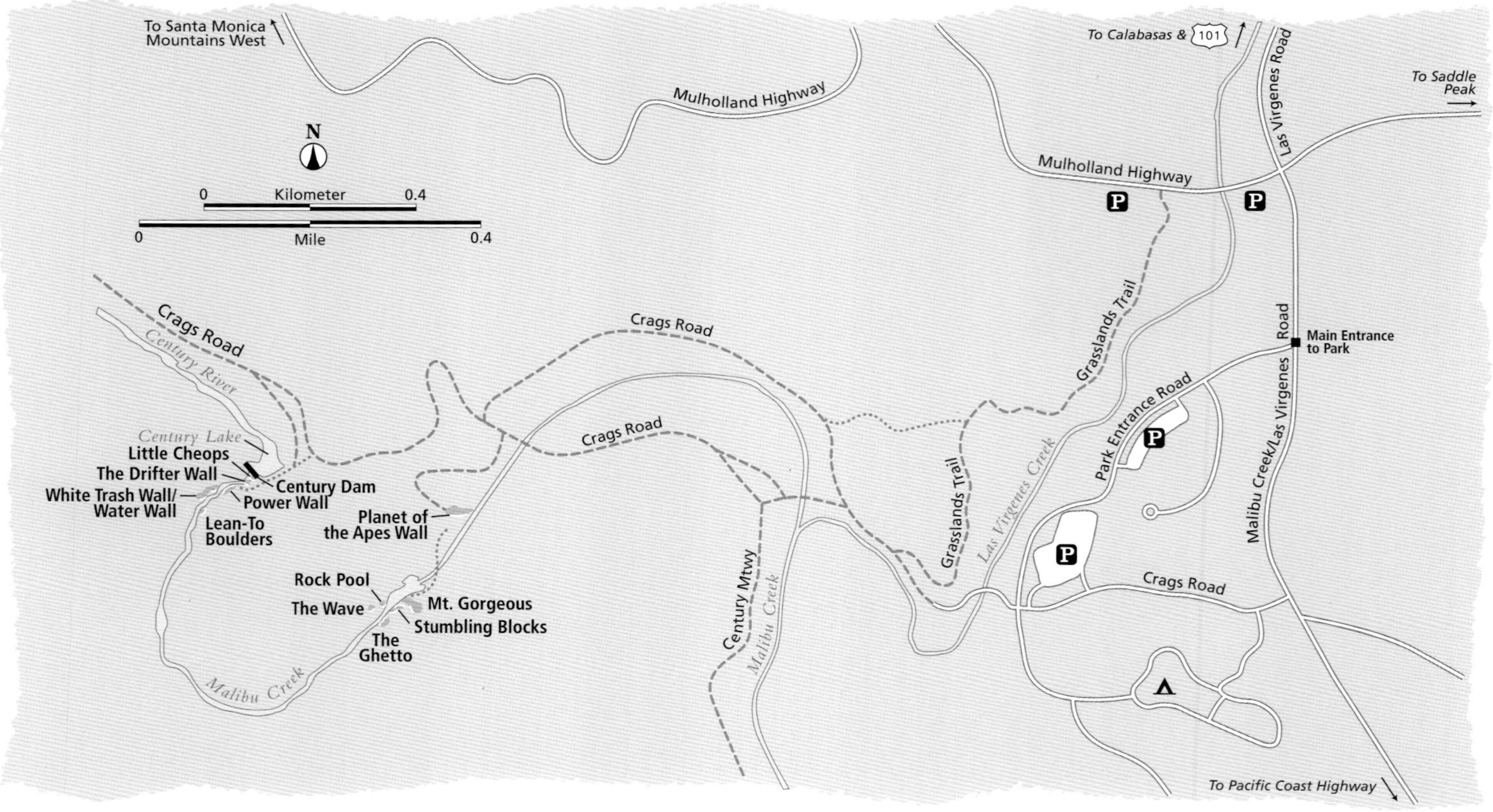

5.

Malibu Creek State Park

The fire road to the cliffs of Malibu Creek was built in the early 1900s and led to the now torn down Crags Club Lodge, where wealthy families once came to experience wilderness in an upscale manner. Soon after the lodge's closure in the 1930s, 20th Century Fox, Paramount Pictures, and President Ronald Reagan all became a part of Malibu Creek's history, purchasing parts of the park and constructing huge movie ranches. The movie ranches helped produce such films as the original Tarzan series, the Planet of the Apes series, *Butch Cassidy and the Sundance Kid*, and the famous army comedy *M.A.S.H.*

The climbing history here began in the 1980s with a group of locals putting the word out that the volcanic rock of Malibu Creek was bad, in theory giving them plenty of time to pick the gems for themselves. One of the locals, Dave Katz, made 200 copies of a small guidebook—*Getting High in L.A.*—that brought the first bit of attention to Malibu Creek. Dave bolted the first sport route at The Ghetto in 1985, and development continued on this wall until Shawn Diamond's addition in 2002, Lateralus, the hardest route in the park. In 1994

Jack Marshall visited Malibu Creek and put up some of the most classic lines on the already popular Planet of the Apes Wall, opening climbers' eyes to the routes that had yet to be climbed and paving the way for more development throughout the park.

The late 1990s and early 2000s saw Malibu hit the map, and development spread throughout the narrow canyon and up its even smaller and tighter side canyons. The Century Dam area was developed during this time and helped spread the crowds around the park more evenly. Many climbers committed days and weeks of their lives along with money out of their own pockets to continue developing the park—people like Bill Leventhal, Matt Oliphant, Mike Draper, Louie Anderson, John Long, and John Mireles. Be aware that bolting is currently off-limits in the park.

Getting there: From the north take US 101, exit at Las Virgenes Road, and head south toward the ocean. Drive 3.2 miles to Mulholland Highway and turn right at the light. There is a small dirt lot immediately on the left, or after another 0.2 mile there is ample parking off both sides of the road near the entrance to the

Grasslands Trail. The main entrance of Malibu Creek State Park is 0.2 mile past Mulholland Highway on your right. (A fee is charged to park inside the state park.)

From the west take the Pacific Coast Highway (PCH)/CA 1 for 11.8 miles east of Decker Canyon Road (CA 23) and turn left onto Malibu Canyon Road/Las Virgenes Road. Follow this road for 6.1 miles to the state park entrance where there is pay parking, or continue 0.2 mile to Mulholland Highway and turn left at the light to the pullouts listed above.

From the junction of the PCH and I-10, drive 12.8 miles northwest and turn right onto Malibu Canyon Road/ Las Virgenes Road. Follow the directions above to the parking areas.

Finding the crag: From the state park parking lot, follow signs for Crags Road and cross a bridge. After 0.2 mile you will come to a fork in the road; take the left fork for Crags Road. Pass the visitor center on your left and cross a second bridge, then take a left onto a dirt path following signs to the Rock Pool. The Planet of the Apes Wall is on your right. To reach Century Lake Canyon, continue straight after crossing the second bridge and follow the signs for Crags Road and Century Lake.

From the free parking on Mulholland Highway, hike the Grasslands Trail, staying to the right when it forks at the top of a hill. After 0.7 mile you will reach the Crags Road Trail, and at

about 1.5 miles you'll come to a fork in the dirt road. For the Planet of the Apes area, take the left fork and then take a right at the port-o-potty. Walk for another minute; the wall is on your right. For the Century Lake Canyon area, take the right fork and hike the dirt road for another 0.5 mile to the Century Lake Canyon climber's trail at the dam.

PLANET OF THE APES WALL

This hugely popular toprope wall can get crowded, but the climbing is excellent and worth the wait. Scenes from *Planet of the Apes* and *M.A.S.H.* were filmed here along with countless other commercials and movies.

Finding the crag: This is the first wall you will encounter at the park from the main trail. To access the top, hike up a small trail around the backside. There are many bolts and anchors along the top; bring long slings.

Christmas Pump, 5.10a

Start on the left side of the wall under some large huecos. Climb up to a ledge in a hueco, then get pumped racing to the top.

Spider Monkey, 5.11b

This route starts several feet to the right of Christmas Pump on a series of small pockets. Make bouldery moves through a low crux to a sloping hueco in the bulge. Climb through the bulge to the left and continue on easier terrain to the top.

The view from Mt. Olympus

Planet of the Apes Wall

Planet of the Apes, 5.11a

One of the most popular routes and the original line on the wall. Start to the right of Spider Monkey, in the corner, and climb to a large hueco above the small roof. Traverse left from here on awesome gym-like features and finish up the top part of Spider Monkey.

Gorilla of My Dreams (aka Leftist Gorilla), 5.12a

This route starts 5 feet to the right of Planet of the Apes, around the corner. Climb up and to the right on small pockets toward a huge flake. Follow the flake up and left toward the upper wall and overhang.

Guerilla Warfare, 5.12a

This fun variation starts 8 feet right of Gorilla of my Dreams and climbs up a series of pockets to the flake where you join Gorilla.

Monkey Sang, Monkey Do, 5.11c

This route starts 10 feet to the right of Guerilla Warfare. Start on the left side of the large depression in the wall and climb up right to a small roof feature. Climb up and left to finish on fun terrain through the overhang.

STUMBLING BLOCKS

The Stumbling Blocks were developed in the late 1990s mostly by Matt Oliphant and Bill Leventhal. This is a great spot to spend an afternoon due to the continuous shade around the blocks. It also boasts a good range of climbs for everyone.

Finding the crag: From the Planet of the Apes Wall, continue down the trail and take one of the small trails across the creek to a dirt path on the opposite side. Follow this path to the right toward the large swimming hole. You will come to an apron of rock that runs down into the creek; traverse this on easy terrain until you need to stem across a wide gap and turn a corner (the crux). Continue alongside the creek; once the terrain opens up you will see the Stumbling Blocks up on your left. Guerilla Drilla is up to the left and Chopping Block is up to the right. Access the routes by scrambling up the large boulder on the right.

The origin of the creek's name likely derives from the Chumash name U-mali-wu, which means "it makes a loud noise there." The Spanish recorded this as Malibu. Actor and activist Bob Hope donated a majority of the land in the park; his philanthropy has helped to preserve this 8,200-acre gem.

Chopping Block, 5.8

This route is on the west face and starts precariously on top of a boulder. A series of good pockets and flakes leads to an excellent viewpoint from the top. 8 bolts with 2 rap rings.

Vigilante, 5.10d

Start just to the right of Chopping Block, on top of a pointed boulder; you can clip the first bolt from here. Climb up and slightly right over the arch on pockets and edges. 4 bolts to 2 open shuts and 1 chain.

Nikki Reardon gets some exposure on Chopping Block (5.8) at the Stumbling Blocks in Malibu Creek.

The Third Degree, 5.10b

The next route to the left of Guerilla Drilla, this was the first route bolted at the Stumbling Blocks. A spooky start onto the block leads to good holds heading slightly left at first. Finish up the ever-steepening headwall to the anchors. 4 bolts to 1 bolt and 2 open shuts.

Guerilla Drilla, 5.10a

Start in the middle of the north face on the slab and head up and to the right. The first part is easy climbing on good edges and huecos, leading to a steep face and a short overhang. 5 bolts to 2 chains.

Stumbling Blocks

Stumbling Blocks

Letterbox

Nipple Denial
Syndrome

Mr. Big

Mr. Big, 5.10d

This climb is on the South Block and starts on the right side as you approach from The Third Degree. Climb large flakes and huecos to a traversing arête, then climb up and left to the anchors. 6 bolts to 2 closed shuts.

Nipple Denial Syndrome, 5.11b

This route and Letterbox start just left of the arête, around the corner from Mr. Big. After clipping the first bolt, climb up and right toward the large hueco. Climb over the small bulge and finish up the arête to the same anchors as Mr. Big. 5 bolts to 2 closed shuts.

Letterbox, 5.11c

This climb shares the same start as Nipple Denial Syndrome, but after the first bolt, climb up and left into the short overhang. Grab the namesake Letterbox hold and climb over the bulge. Finish up the easier headwall. 4 bolts to 2 closed shuts.

Blockbuster, 5.11a

Around the corner to the left of the South Block routes. Start to the right of the arête on a boulder, then climb through pockets straight up to the arête and follow the arête to the anchors up and right. There are lots of hidden jugs around the back of the arête. 5 bolts to 1 open shut and 1 chain.

Stumbling Blocks

Blockbuster

MT. GORGEOUS

This is a great wall with long moderates, and the left overhanging flank has some harder lines. The base of the wall stays shady most of the day, while the upper headwall only sees shade in the early morning.

Finding the crag: Follow the steep climber's trail that begins at the base of The Third Degree. Hike uphill and scramble through some boulders to get to the base of the wall. The following climbs are on the south face.

Gorgeous, 5.10a

Start at the bottom of the pink streak on a slab with good pockets, then climb to a natural rest below a small roof. The crux comes pulling over the bulge; finish up the headwall to the anchors. 7 bolts to 2 open shuts. 60 feet.

Family Jewel, 5.10c

Start to the right of Gorgeous on a less than vertical section and climb toward a huge morphed hueco in the wall. Climb around the left side of the feature to steep jugs, then pull a crux move over a small roof. 8 bolts to 3 open shuts. 50 feet.

Delicious, 5.10d

Climb up and left on a slightly less than vertical section of the wall to the same morphed hueco as on Family Jewel. Climb up the right side of the feature this time and continue climbing on good flakes and pockets to a crux bulge followed by easier climbing to the anchors. 10 bolts to 2 chains.

Remains from the set of the TV show *M.A.S.H.* can be seen farther down Crags Road. Continue hiking for another mile past the entrance to the climbs in the Century Dam area.

Delicious

Family Jewel

Gorgeous

Rock Pool

Hot Lips

ROCK POOL

The Rock Pool has several good boulder problems and the popular highball/toprope route, Hot Lips.

Finding the boulder: From the Stumbling Blocks, walk past Blockbuster on your right and follow the creek, cross to the other side when you can, and look for this stand-alone boulder. Access the anchors on top by scrambling up the backside.

Hot Lips, 5.12a/V5

Climb up large huecos and make a long move to a baseball-size hole, then climb left to a huge hueco where you can take a rest. Climb through the crux and top out to the left.

Pick your poison: highball or toprope? Shawn Diamond rolls the dice sans the rope on Hot Lips (5.12a/V5).

THE GHETTO

The Ghetto hosts a series of deep caves that have excellent moderates and the hardest climbs in the park. This was the first major wall developed for lead climbing in the park back in the mid-1980s to early 1990s, with the most difficult routes added by Shawn Diamond in the early 2000s. The cliff gets shade in the morning and late afternoon. The routes are between 30 and 60 feet in length.

Finding the crag: From the Hot Lips boulder continue up the creek. In dry seasons you can cross the creek on your left by scrambling over some river rocks to where the cliff meets the creek, then hike along the edge of the creek to access the Ghetto wall. In rainy seasons when the creek is higher, you may have to stay on the right side of the creek when you walk past Hot Lips. Follow the cliff to a serious rock traverse over and around the creek; the Ghetto wall will be at your back.

Skeezer Pleaser, 5.11b

The route starts right above the water on the left of the first cave and leads right into steep climbing on good holds. Find a good rest in the large hueco. The crux comes when you pull onto the final slab. 5 bolts to 2 open shuts.

Kathmandu, 5.10b

This next route to the right was the first route bolted at the Ghetto. Climb steep pockets and jugs up to the right

The Ghetto

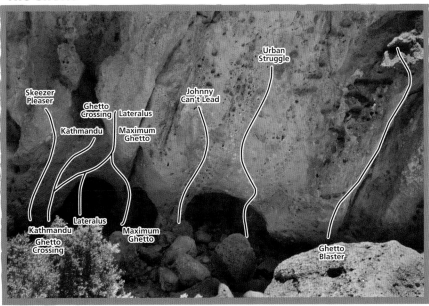

to the base of a large cave. 4 bolts to 2 chains.

Ghetto Crossing, 5.13a

This linkup climbs right over the main cave and features consistent climbing on small pockets and edges with no real rests. Start the same as Kathmandu, but after clipping the second bolt begin climbing to the right over the cave for one bolt, then join the last five bolts of Lateralus. 8 bolts to 2 chains.

Lateralus, 5.14a

The hardest route in the park starts in the deepest part of the first cave. Climb up flakes and pockets in the back of the cave and then climb left along the roof toward the mouth of the cave. The bouldery crux comes as you exit the cave on small pockets. Clip the fourth bolt, then head to the right for four more bolts to the anchors. 8 bolts to 2 chains. For an easier variation (Brenna, 5.13d), finish at the anchors for Kathmandu in the cave on your left after the fifth bolt.

Maximum Ghetto, 5.13a

Climb the pillar with interesting features on the right side of the first cave. Climb up and to the left over the mouth of the cave using a mono along the way. After clipping the third bolt, head right to the anchors of Lateralus and Ghetto Crossing. 6 bolts to 2 chains. For an easier variation (Stun Gun, 5.12d), finish at the anchors for Kathmandu.

Johnny Can't Lead, 5.11b

An outstanding steep endurance jug haul that was one of the two original lines bolted at the Ghetto. Climb up the pillar between the second and third caves on large holds. Follow the line of pockets up to the right with a couple of good rests. Make a big move left off the broken block before the anchors. 5 bolts to 2 open shuts.

Urban Struggle, 5.12b

This route starts on the right side of the third cave. Start on the inside of the cave and climb up to a rail; traverse it right out of the cave. Stand up on the rail and make some long moves on good pockets directly up and to the left. After clipping the fourth bolt, climb to the right through easier terrain to the anchors. 6 bolts to 2 chains.

Ghetto Blaster, 5.13b

This classic lies around the corner from the main caves. Start on the smooth apron of rock and climb up past the rail to a good hueco. Climb to the right for a few moves to another good hueco you can clip from. Climb straight up to a good rest, then head left toward the water streaks. Find one more good rest before the final boulder problem over the bulge. 7 bolts to 2 chains.

THE WAVE

This hidden wall is a great escape on busy summer days and offers shade all afternoon.

Finding the crag: From the Ghetto wall follow the large boulders up the creek and eventually cross to the opposite side. You'll see a free-standing boulder with too many bolts running up it; walk around the left side and hike up the hillside. There are fixed ropes to help with the hike up the canyon; follow them for another 5 minutes to the base of the wall.

Amphetamine, 5.11b

Just to the right of the arête, climb directly up with some long moves on pockets and edges to the fifth bolt, then climb left a little to clip the anchors or head right toward the large hueco and finish at the anchors for Pocket Jones. 5 bolts to an open shut and chain.

Pocket Jones, 5.11c

Start right of Amphetamine. Climb up over a small overlap and make some long moves up thin pockets with the occasional rest in a good hueco. 6 bolts to 2 open shuts.

Pocket Pool, 5.11c

Start next to the white streak at the base of the wall and follow thin pockets. This route is less reachy than Pocket Jones. 5 bolts to open shuts.

CENTURY LAKE CANYON

This area is in the back of the park and sees a lot less traffic than some of the other popular cliffs.

Finding the crag: From the main trail on Crags Road (after walking uphill for 0.5 mile from the fork), look for a side trail on your left with the sign, "No Bikes on Trail." Follow this for 0.1 mile to a fence. Climb around the side of the fence over the water, and then climb over the dam and the fence. You will be standing above and to the left of Little Cheops. Follow the trail straight ahead and to the left a little, then scramble down and to the right by climbing down past a tree at the top of a little dihedral. Follow the dihedral down and around to the right to the base of the Drifter Wall.

The Wave

Amphetamine   Pocket Jones   Pocket Pool

THE DRIFTER WALL

This tall, steep wall hosts the best 5.12 in the park—The Drifter—put up by Louie Anderson.

Finding the crag: This is the first wall you arrive at when entering Century Canyon.

The Drifter, 5.12a

Start on the left side near the corner and climb up on good pockets to a large hueco under the roof at the second bolt. Traverse to the right and follow the bolts out of the roof heading toward the right. Continue on thin pockets and edges up to the right to the shared anchors under the roof. 7 bolts to 2 open shuts.

Fallout, 5.11c

The farthest line to the right on the main wall. Climb up on small edges and pockets through some bouldery cruxes before joining The Drifter for its final two bolts. 4 bolts to 2 open shuts.

Fallout

The Drifter

LITTLE CHEOPS

This secluded wall offers some great short warm-ups and toprope opportunities that are usually in the shade until early afternoon.

Finding the crag: The wall is between the Drifter Wall and the dam. From the Drifter Wall scramble through the notch to the right of the wall or, if the water is low, scramble around through a cave to the left.

Scarab, 5.9

Climb up through some large huecos on a vertical face, occasionally using the arête when needed. Finish up and left at the anchors. 5 bolts to 1 open and 1 closed shut.

Tut, 5.10b

About 10 feet to the left of Scarab. Climb on good pockets and large huecos that lead to a crux with a long reach in the middle. Continue straight up to the anchors. 4 bolts to 1 open and 1 closed shut.

Tut

Scarab

POWER WALL

This is another great beginner's wall that gets morning shade. A couple of fun 5.9s are on the right set of anchors. Belay from the boulder in the creek.

Finding the crag: From the Drifter Wall walk down the creek away from the dam and cross on boulders in the middle of the creek. The Power Wall, with its fluted features and large huecos, is visible on your left. Scramble over to the belay boulder at the base of the wall.

Power Station, 5.10b

This route is the easier start to Rolling Blackout and starts at the base of the large scooped-out dihedral, climbing up and right following a series of huecos with lots of good stemming. 6 bolts to 1 open shut and 1 chain.

Rolling Blackout, 5.10d

This slightly harder start is just 8 feet to the right of Power Station. Climb up and left through two bulges, then clip the third bolt to join the top of Power Station. 6 bolts to 1 open shut and 1 chain.

Power Wall

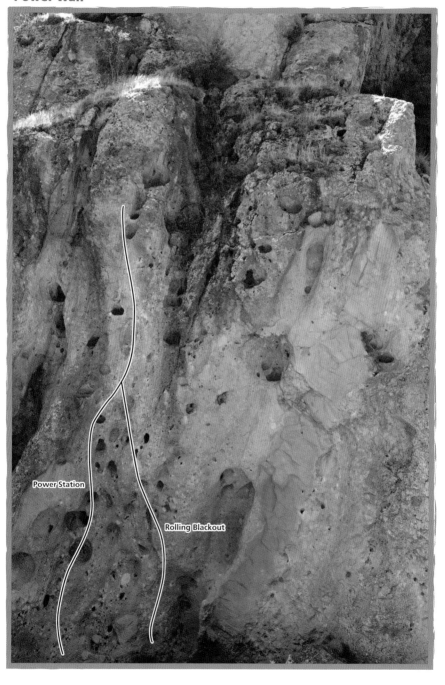

Power Station

Rolling Blackout

WATER WALL AND WHITE TRASH WALL

These two walls were developed by Louie Anderson and offer a great variety of climbing away from the crowds.

Finding the crag: The two walls are on the opposite side of the creek from the Power Wall and can be accessed by going directly across the stream from the Power Wall. The Water Wall is on your right, and you can see the Fissure Man crack. The White Trash Wall is just downstream and around the corner and is noticeable for its huge overhanging belly at mid-height.

Fissure Man, 5.10c

Start on the left slab with good pockets, then climb to the upper headwall where the crack begins; follow the crack and jugs to the top of the wall. 6 bolts to 2 open shuts.

Water Boy, 5.10c

The harder start to Fissure Man begins to the right on the slightly overhanging wall in the pit. Climb up good pockets and edges to get established on the upper headwall, then traverse left to join Fissure Man. 8 bolts to 2 open shuts.

White Trash, 5.13a

This is the leftmost route on the White Trash Wall and goes through the steepest part of the wall with the crux deadpoint move coming out of the roof. Good edges follow the roof to the anchors. 7 bolts to 2 open shuts.

Trailer Trash, 5.12b

This is a linkup that climbs most of Trailer Park, then finishes by traversing left at the huge hueco and joining White Trash at its final two bolts. 8 bolts to 2 open shuts.

Trailer Park, 5.11a

Start down in a little pit and climb up good pockets. Make a transition left onto the main headwall, then follow the arête to the top. 5 bolts to 2 open shuts.

Water Wall and White Trash Wall

LEAN-TO BOULDERS

Two oversize "boulders" lean on each other and form a dark chasm containing a super-classic John Long route, Swamp Thing.

Finding the boulders: From the White Trash Wall you can see the Lean-to Boulders across the creek and downstream just a little. Scramble over to get to the base of the boulders.

Swamp Thing (aka Pit and the Pendulum), 5.12c

This route is on the right side of the main overhanging boulder. Start down in the pit (there might be water). Climb up through steep technical pockets to the right toward the arête. The climbing gets slightly easier after that—the route climbs like a long boulder problem. 5 bolts to 1 open shut and 1 chain.

Lean-to Boulders

Swamp Thing

Santa Monica sunset colors

Santa Monica Mountains West

The western portion of the Santa Monica Mountains offers some amazing climbing opportunities chock full of stunning Pacific Ocean views and hidden cliffs deep in the Santa Monica backcountry. Follow the Mishe Mokwe Trail or the Sandstone Peak trails out to Echo Cliffs and the Backcountry Crags for some unforgettable climbing locations. Echo offers some of the longest single-pitch routes in SoCal, along with some amazing testpieces. You will find Echo Cliffs to be a bit busier on weekends, but you can always escape the crowds by hitting up one of the many satellite areas: The Lookout, The Hueco Wall, Mount Olympus, or Boney Bluff.

There are great camping opportunities on the Pacific Coast Highway 1 at Leo Carrillo, just 1.9 miles south of the junction at Yerba Buena Road. After a great day of climbing, you can be sure to find a hearty fresh-caught seafood meal at the locals' favorite Neptune's Net, at the junction of the Pacific Coast Highway 1 and Yerba Buena Road.

Santa Monica Mountains West

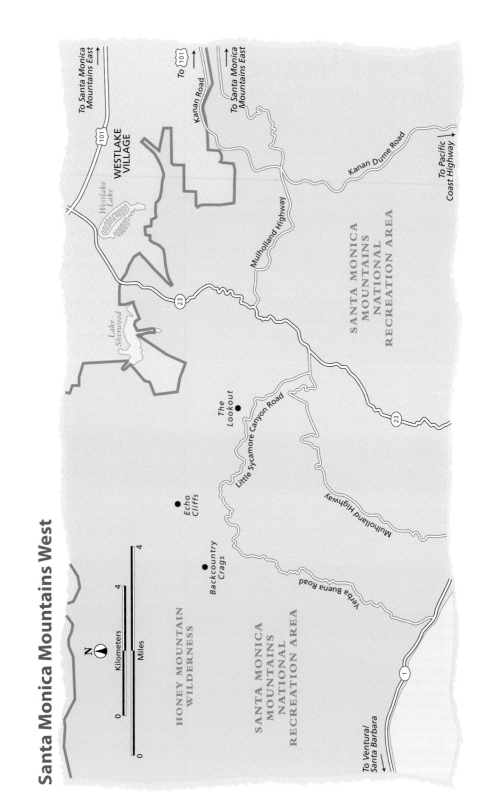

6.

The Lookout

The Lookout is a great place for moderate climbing on short routes. The approach is short, unlike some of the major crags in the Santa Monica Mountains, and the view is spectacular—try to catch a sunset here; you won't regret it.

Darshan Etz and Abe (last name unknown) originally bolted toprope anchors at The Lookout. Later, Louie Anderson saw the sport climbing potential for this small volcanic breccia crag and in the early 2000s developed the popular routes on the west face. Development has been restricted to the main formation only due to rockfall potential onto the road, so please be aware of your surroundings while climbing here.

Getting there: From the north take US 101 and exit at Westlake Boulevard/CA 23. Follow Westlake Boulevard south for 7.6 miles and take a right onto Mulholland Highway. Drive 0.4 mile and take a right onto Little Sycamore Canyon Road. After 2.3 miles you'll see a dirt pullout on your left; park here.

From the south follow the Pacific Coast Highway (PCH) northwest for 24.7 miles from the junction with I-10, then take a right onto Decker Canyon Road/CA 23 North. Follow this road for 4.7 miles, then take a left onto Mulholland Highway; follow the directions above to the parking area.

Finding the crag: From the parking area, cross the street and head back south down the road for 0.1 mile. At the sharp right turn you'll pass a paved fire road on your left; just past this is a thicket of bushes on your left. Look for a break in the bushes and head up a dirt footpath. Hike up the small ridge for a few minutes until you come to a large boulder. At the boulder a side trail makes a sharp right into a small gully; follow this over some rocks and alongside the main formation. The trail drops steeply to the right and eventually turns left to the bottom of the main crag. 10-minute walk.

Espionage, 5.10c
The second line of bolts in from the left on the main crag's west face. Climb up good edges and sidepulls (easier once you know where the good holds are). 3 bolts to open shuts.

Double Agent, 5.10a
The line to the right of Espionage. Start beneath a huge, broken gray

The Lookout

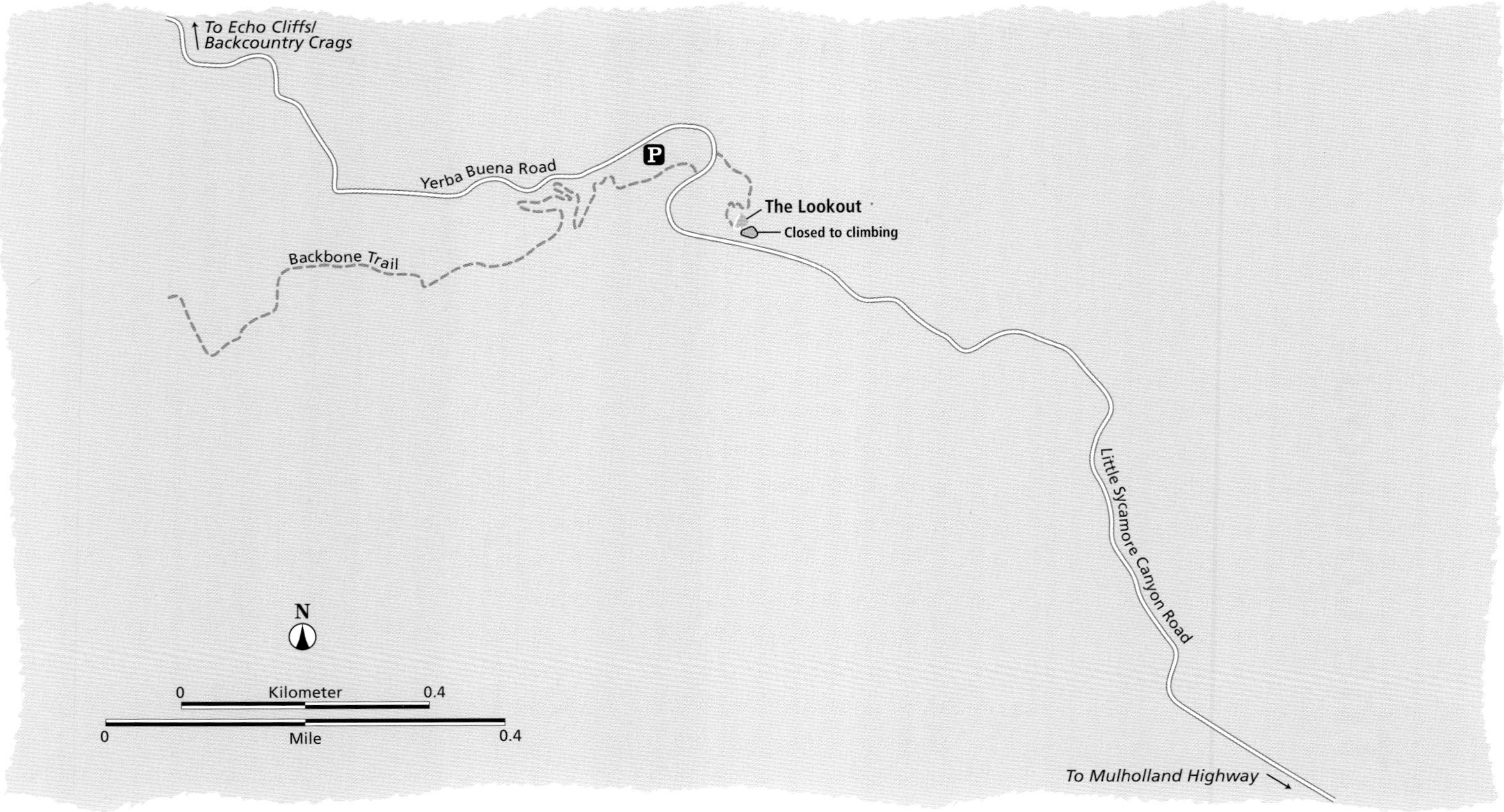

To Echo Cliffs/
Backcountry Crags

Yerba Buena Road

P

Backbone Trail

The Lookout
Closed to climbing

Little Sycamore Canyon Road

To Mulholland Highway

N

Kilometer
0   0.4

Mile
0   0.4

rock and climb up edges toward the roof, then get a good rest before the crux bulge. Larger holds lead to the anchors. 4 bolts to 2 open shuts.

Hidden Agenda, 5.11b

The next set of bolts to the right of Double Agent. Climb up the shallow grove and head left on small edges with technical moves. The climbing gets easier near the top where you climb the same bulge as on Double Agent. 4 bolts to 2 open shuts.

Eye to the Sky, 5.11b

The next line of bolts to the right of Hidden Agenda, just right of the shallow grove. Climb straight up through edges and some good liebacks to the dihedral at the summit. 5 bolts to 2 open shuts.

Incognito, 5.11b

The last line of bolts on the main west face. Climb up the face left of the arête until the top, then use the arête for the final bulge. 6 bolts to 2 open shuts.

Conspiracy, 5.12a (no topo)

This is the first climb around the corner from Incognito, on the south face. Pre-clip the first bolt due to the low crux being a potential ground fall hazard. Follow the awesome arête with sustained climbing to the top. 5 bolts to 2 open shuts.

The Lookout

The Santa Monica Mountains are riddled with spectacular views; Victor Ramirez finds one while climbing Incognito (5.11b) at The Lookout.

Echo Cliffs

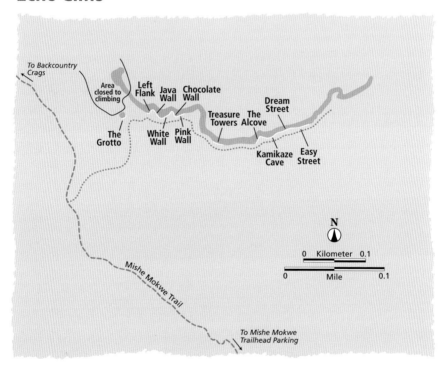

To Backcountry Crags

Area closed to climbing

Left Flank

Java Wall

Chocolate Wall

Dream Street

Treasure Towers

The Alcove

The Grotto

White Wall

Pink Wall

Kamikaze Cave

Easy Street

N

| 0 | Kilometer | 0.1 |

| 0 | Mile | 0.1 |

Mishe Mokwe Trail

To Mishe Mokwe Trailhead Parking

7.

Echo Cliffs

Tucked deep in a valley of the inner Santa Monica Mountains, Echo Cliffs offers climbers everything from the longest moderate single-pitch routes in LA on the Java Wall, to the horizontal roof of the Kamikaze Cave, to the long, easy multipitch climbs at Easy Street. The Santa Monica Mountains offer a huge variety of flora along the hike in to the crag and at the base of the cliff line. One plant in particular, the Dudleya succulent, is an endangered species found growing near the stream in the Grotto. Any climbs upstream of Game Boy or the Superfly wall have been closed to climbing. Please help keep this area open by staying on route, being aware of the flora near routes, and always picking up your trash.

Development at Echo Cliffs began in 1994. Louie Anderson and Jack Marshall were contacted by local trail runner Jeff Willis, who had spotted the huge cliffs after a wildfire ripped through the area in the early 1990s. Louie and Jack were so thoroughly impressed with the vast amount of good volcanic breccia and the height of the walls that they immediately returned to start bolting routes. The crew put a lot of time and effort into building belay patios and trails along the base of the cliffs and to each individual crag. There is also a series of rebar ladders to access the farther reaches of the cliffs. Please be respectful and stay on established trails.

Many of the routes at Echo are long, so come to this crag with a 60-meter rope and long slings. Use your own quickdraws or carabiners for toproping, as many of the anchors are getting thin from overuse. Fall through spring is the best time to visit this crag; the summer can be quite hot unless you make it in for an early morning or early evening session. The walls go in and out of the sun throughout the day due to the multiple directions they face.

For some outstanding authentic tacos, tortas, and burritos, head over to Thousand Oaks on the way out and check out Badass Tacos on East Thousand Oaks Boulevard.

Getting there: From the north take US 101 and exit at Westlake Boulevard (CA 23). Follow Westlake Boulevard south for 7.6 miles and take a right onto Mulholland Highway. Drive 0.4 mile and take a right onto Little Sycamore Canyon Road. After 3.9 miles you'll see a dirt parking lot for the Mishe Mokwe Trailhead on your left; park here.

Less than ten years after putting up his first route, Louie Anderson's passion for development, along with the help of Steve Edwards, Jack Marshall, and Doniel Drazien, has resulted in well over 150 documented routes—up to 5.14b—at Echo Cliffs.

From the south follow the Pacific Coast Highway (PCH)/CA 1 northwest for 24.7 miles from the junction with I-10, then take a right onto Decker Canyon Road/CA 23 North. Follow this road for 4.7 miles, then take a left onto Mulholland Highway; follow the directions above to the parking area.

Finding the crag: From the parking area, cross the street and start hiking on the Mishe Mokwe Trail. After 0.6 mile you'll see a trail sign on your left for the Backbone Trail; stay on the main trail. At around 1.5 miles descend a wide section of trail into a gully. There is a water drainage to your right; follow this down to the cliff base (you will be in the Grotto section of Echo Cliffs).

THE GROTTO

The Grotto is a great place to stop first and warm up on some shorter and easier climbs. Climbing upstream from the routes listed in this book is prohibited due to the endangered succulent growing there. The routes here are about 40 feet long.

Finding the crag: Once you arrive at the base of the gully, Miss Pacman and Game Boy are on the freestanding wall on your left.

Miss Pacman, 5.8

This route goes up the middle of the wall. Start just to the right of the tree growing from around the corner. Climb up and right to the first bolt, then straight up the nice face to the anchors. 5 bolts to 2 open shuts.

Game Boy, 5.9

The right arête on the wall. Start off a boulder in the stream and work your way through the tricky beginning. Continue up the arête past five bolts, then traverse up and left to the anchors shared with Miss Pacman. 5 bolts to 2 open shuts.

LEFT FLANK

The Left Flank gets lots of sun and is a great warm-up wall before jumping on the sustained walls nearby. The routes here are about 90 feet long, excluding Bushed Coyote, which is about 60 feet long.

Finding the crag: When you arrive at the base of the gully, walk toward the cliff line and follow it to the right around the corner. The Left Flank is the main wall on your left.

Bushed Coyote, 5.11a

The route follows the left side of the arête on the far left of the wall. Climb through powerful, bouldery moves in the bottom to access the arête. Follow this to the top and finish on a nice crack. 5 bolts to 2 open shuts.

Morning Glory, 5.9

The first route to the right of the main crack down the middle of the wall. Start left of the tree in the trail and climb up the slab, occasionally using the crack, then finish to the right of the bush growing out of the top of the wall. 9 bolts to 2 ring anchors.

B-Line, 5.10a

The second route to the left of the wall's far right starts left of the black water streak (Black Tide). Good climbing up the slabs leads to the vertical headwall with the crux going to the anchors. 9 bolts to 2 open shuts.

Black Tide, 5.9

Start under the black water streak and climb up the face on good holds to an easier slab at mid-height. Continue up to the corner and stem to the anchors. 12 bolts to 2 ring anchors.

JAVA WALL

This is the major wall in sight for most of the hike down the final gully into Echo Cliff. The Java Wall is one of the most popular moderate walls at the entire cliff. The routes here are long (all about 100 feet) and require lots of endurance.

Finding the crag: Java Wall is directly to the right of Left Flank.

Espresso, 5.11a

The leftmost route on the wall. Start on a slab with good flakes and pockets up to a ramp. Climb left to the next bolt then straight up to the bottom of the arête. Pulling around the bulge and onto the arête is the crux. Continue climbing the left line of bolts on good holds up steep and pumpy terrain to the anchors. Climb the right line of bolts after the bulge for a 5.11c finish. 12 bolts to 3 open shuts.

Caffeine, 5.11b

The next set of bolts to the right of Espresso. Climb up an easy ramp, passing three bolts to a set of anchors; continue climbing through the technical crux in the black water streak on the left line of bolts. After clipping five more bolts, follow the right line of bolts next to the dihedral up and right to the anchors. 12 bolts to 2 open shuts.

Java, 5.11d

The second route over from the right arête and a very popular one for the grade. Climb through a faint water streak on pockets and edges through a technical crux at the fourth bolt. After the eighth bolt gain a good ledge before the final pumpy head-wall. 12 bolts to 2 open shuts.

WHITE WALL AND CHOCOLATE WALL

The White Wall hosts one of the largest concentrations of long (80 to 100 feet), hard (5.12 and 5.13) routes, and the Chocolate Wall has one of the best 5.10s at the cliff.

Finding the crags: The White Wall is the overhanging wall just around the corner from the Java Wall. The Chocolate Wall is the dark brown wall just to the right.

The Hunger, 5.12d

The first route on the left-hand side of the wall. Climb to the ledge and a high first bolt, then continue up the amazing sustained face on pockets and edges. Climb past four more bolts to a set of anchors (the end of Choptop, 5.12c), then continue to the left around the arête past five more bolts to the anchors on the right side of the Java Wall. 10 bolts to 2 open shuts.

State of Grace, 5.13b

The next line to the right of The Hunger. Climb up the ledge and onto the face past two bolts and a small roof before the third bolt. Continue up the overhanging face following the line of fixed draws toward the black water

White Wall and Chocolate Wall

Bob Passerini past the crux on State of Grace (5.13b) at the White Wall at Echo Cliffs.

streak. Traverse left to the anchors after the last bolt. 8 bolts to 2 open shuts.

The Power of One, 5.13d

The next route to the right, Power of One starts on the same ledge system and climbs up the line of fixed draws. Climb through amazing edges, pockets, pinches, and lieback flakes on this severely overhanging route. The crux comes near the top with a difficult deadpoint move. 10 bolts to 3 open shuts.

The Stand, 5.12d

The fourth line of bolts from the left of the wall. Start in the orange-streaked rock below The Power of One's ledge system and climb up the arête through two cruxes toward a big hole on the right. Climb past the hole to easier terrain on the upper headwall. 10 bolts to 2 open shuts.

The Stain, 5.12b

The fifth route in from the left side of the wall. Climb up the prominent black water streak into the bouldery crux at the third bolt, then continue up the easier headwall, passing the large hole to your left; the anchors are below the left corner in the roof. 7 bolts to 2 open shuts.

Calm, 5.12a

Start up the slab for three bolts on the far left side of the Chocolate Wall. Climb up the overhanging fin of rock, then follow the bolts through good edges and protrusions through a crux near the top. 9 bolts to 2 open shuts.

Death by Chocolate, 5.10d

Most people stick-clip the first bolt for safety. Start under the roof and make a hard exit to gain the main face—very bouldery up to the third bolt. Finish up the face on easier but sustained terrain to the anchors. 8 bolts to 2 open shuts.

PINK WALL

The glowing Pink Wall has some incredible rock and long (80 to 100 feet) intermediate routes.

Finding the crag: The Pink Wall is just around the corner from the Chocolate Wall.

Pretty in Pink, 5.12a

The first route on the left side of the wall. Climb up the face to the right of the arête on thin edges leading to the endurance crux near the anchors. 9 bolts to 2 chain anchors.

Split Decision, 5.11d

The next route to the right of Pretty in Pink. Start up the easy face through two bolts, then continue on the left line of bolts to a technical crux at the third bolt and edges up the pumpy headwall. 10 bolts to 2 open shuts.

Restrain This, 5.11c

This route shares the same start as Split Decision. After clipping the second bolt, follow the right line of bolts, making long moves on good holds to get through the lower crux. Continue climbing up and to the right on easier terrain. 8 bolts to 2 chain anchors.

Meager and Weak, 5.12c

The first line of bolts to the left of the large boulder at the base of the wall. After clipping the first bolt, continue climbing through a technical crux to the line of bolts on the right. Get a good rest after the fifth bolt, then race the pump to the anchors with a good variety of holds along the way. 9 bolts to 3 open shuts.

Terror in New York, 5.10d

Climb up the right side of the formation through a bouldery crux on big holds. Clip a tricky third bolt, then climb through thin edges on the vertical face to access the upper slab. 7 bolts to 2 open shuts.

TREASURE TOWERS

This area often gets overlooked because the cobbles look chossy; on the contrary, the routes are quite solid and offer great long (80 to 100 feet) moderates.

Finding the crag: From the Pink Wall continue down the main trail to a boulder scramble on the right of the trail. Follow the boulders down to the base of the obvious towers.

Windfall, 5.11a

A hidden gem. Climb the blunt left arête with great exposure that leads to cobble pulling all the way to the crux bulge near the top. 8 bolts to 2 open shuts.

Diamond in the Rough, 5.11b

The next route to the right. Climb the center of the tower through a faint water streak. Get a good rest at the fifth bolt, then continue up left on the steep headwall through four more bolts and easier terrain. 11 bolts to 2 open shuts.

Treasure Towers

THE ALCOVE

Very popular because of the amazing flake climbing on The Guillotine, this wall gets shade in the early morning and afternoon. The routes are about 80 to 100 feet long.

Finding the crag: Continue along the boulders to a downclimb built with a rebar ladder in the rocks and a rope with knots. At the base hike along the main trail for a couple of hundred yards to a large overhang. Walk under the overhang and up a staircase to The Alcove.

Geezer, 5.12a

The third route to the left of the crack (The Guillotine). Start next to the tree and climb up left through the reachy crux at the second bolt; after the third bolt continue straight past a large hueco. Climb through edges up the face to another long move near the top, finishing on the same anchors as The Guillotine. 7 bolts to 2 open shuts.

Pride, 5.13a

The next route to the right of Geezer. Start up the face on thin edges with some reachy moves. Climb to a good rest at the flake, then continue up the main headwall on thin edges with sidepulls and gastons. 9 bolts to 2 open shuts.

The Guillotine, 5.10b

The classic for the area. Climb up the right-leaning crack for two bolts until you can move to the giant hanging flake. Follow the flake up left to the same anchors as Geezer. 8 bolts to 2 open shuts.

The Alcove

KAMIKAZE CAVE

If you are looking for severe horizontal roof climbing, then this is the place for you. The routes here are not long (50 to 80 feet), but are very powerful and dead horizontal for the first few bolts to the upper headwall.

Finding the crag: Crawl through the small hole in the cliff at the far right of The Alcove.

No Remorse, 5.13b

Start on the left side of the light brown formation and climb sloping holds to access the horizontal roof. Climb through a variety of sequences involving underclings, kneebars, pinches, and foot trickery to access the upper headwall where you climb through one more technical crux. 8 bolts to 2 open shuts.

Kamikaze Cave

Crash and Burn

Hijacked

No Remorse

Isamer Bilog on the exit moves of Crash and Burn (5.12d) at Kamikaze Cave.

Crash and Burn, 5.12d

The next route to the right of No Remorse. Climb up the middle of the light brown formation through scoops and slopers. Make big moves on underclings and big pockets with some heel hooks to access the final crux at the lip of the roof. 6 bolts to 2 open shuts.

Hijacked, 5.12c

The farthest route to the right in the cave. Start up the scoops on the light brown rock, then climb through a mono and into the roof. Be cautious clipping the third bolt due to fall potential. Finish the roof on big moves to large pockets. 5 bolts to 2 open shuts.

Dream Street and Easy Street

DREAM STREET AND EASY STREET

Dream Street has some excellent, long 5.12s that get good shade in the afternoon. Easy Street is one of the best places for easy climbing on short or long routes. There are many multipitch sport routes here with lots of variations. The wall gets lots of sun.

Finding the crag: Dream Street is the slightly overhanging wall just down the stairs at the end of the Kamikaze Cave. Easy Street is the major wall just past Dream Street.

Apathy, 5.12d

The second route in from the stone staircase. Start in the corner on top of a rock mound, then climb through the first three bolts on a beautiful gray wall. The crux is through small pockets and tricky feet over the first bulge; this leads to another crux bulge and finally easier terrain. 11 bolts to 2 open shuts.

Immaculate, 5.12a

Start on the steep pocketed wall on the left side of the orange face. Climb past four bolts to a roof, then move up left and past the crux bulge. Sustained climbing on better holds leads to the anchors. 7 bolts to 2 open shuts.

Blackjack, 5.10c

Pitch 1, 5.10b: Start in the black water streak and climb up the steep wall with good holds. Follow this to the right to the water chute. 7 bolts to 2 ring anchors. Pitch 2, 5.10c: Follow the black streak up the vertical face on amazing edges. 7 bolts to 2 ring anchors. Pitch 3, 5.8: Finish the route to the summit by climbing easy terrain on a slab past a small bulge. 7 bolts to 2 ring anchors.

Casey and the Bat, 5.10b

The next line of bolts about 12 feet to the right of Blackjack. Climb the face to the crux pulling over the roof. Continue on the faint water streak to the anchors left of a small dihedral. 12 bolts to 2 open shuts. About 100 feet.

Golden Years, 5.9

Pitch 1, 5.6: About 60 feet down the trail from Casey and the Bat. The climb starts to the right of the large corner in the cliff above. Climb up an easy water chute to a ledge at the anchors. 7 bolts to 2 ring anchors. Pitch 2, 5.9: Climb past the crux bulge and continue up the beautiful golden water streak that wanders slightly to the left over a seam in the wall. 9 bolts to 2 open shuts. About 100 feet.

The Serpent, 5.10a

Pitch 1, 5.6: This route climbs the wide water chute to the right of Golden Years. Ascend the water chute on large holds and good stemming to the first set of anchors. 8 bolts to 2 ring anchors. Pitch 2, 5.10a: Pull the crux bulge onto the easier face above; continue up the bright water streak. 8 bolts to 2 open shuts.

Matt Parent enjoying a sunny day at Echo Cliffs on the first pitch (5.10b) of Black Jack (overall 5.10c)

Righteous Babe, 5.8

Pitch 1, 5.7: Start under the large black water streak to the right of The Serpent. Climb good blocky holds through the water streak to a ledge. 8 bolts to 2 ring anchors. Pitch 2, 5.8: Climb up past the small bulge after the anchors and continue up the black water streak. The top anchors are to the right of the plants growing out of the upper cracks. 8 bolts to 2 open shuts.

Head Wound, 5.9

Climb the first pitch of Righteous Babe, then from the anchors traverse right toward another set of anchors. Climb up the white streak to the amazing and exposed headwall. 9 bolts to 2 open shuts.

8.

Backcountry Crags

The Backcountry Crags take you farther into the heart of the Santa Monica Mountains. Along the trail to Mount Olympus, just below Sandstone Peak's 3,111-foot summit, you will be treated with a sweeping view of the Santa Monica Mountain range, the Pacific coastline, and neighboring islands. The mountains have a Mediterranean climate and see coastal fog on many mornings, which helps the lush environment thrive. There has actually been snow reported on Boney Mountain next to the Boney Bluff climbing area.

Louie Anderson nearly single-handedly developed and claimed the first ascents on almost all the routes at the Hueco Wall and Boney Bluff. Louie's consistent commitment to the long hike, clearing of climber's trails,

and cleaning and bolting of routes is apparent when visiting these satellite areas.

Getting there: From the north take US 101 and exit at Westlake Boulevard/CA 23. Follow Westlake Boulevard south for 7.6 miles and take a right onto Mulholland Highway. Drive 0.4 mile and take a right onto Little Sycamore Canyon Road. After 4.5 miles you'll see a dirt parking lot for the Sandstone Peak Trail/Backbone Trail on your right.

From the south follow the Pacific Coast Highway (PCH)/CA 1 northwest for 24.7 miles from the junction with I-10 and take a right onto Decker Canyon Road/CA 23 North. Follow this road for 4.7 miles, then take a left onto Mulholland Highway; follow the directions above to the parking area.

Backcountry Crags

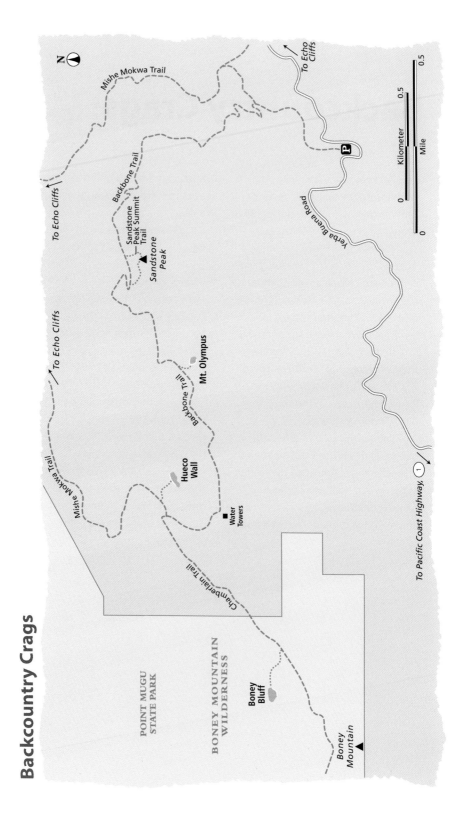

MOUNT OLYMPUS

You will find yourself lost amid a sea of cobbles on your way up the routes on this solitary spire of conglomerate volcanic breccia rock. Fear not, the cobbles have been climbed on since early 2000 when they were first bolted, and there is always a good hold when needed. The view here is a treat, and the easier routes get shade for a good part of the morning and afternoon. The longer routes around the corner get a lot of sun.

Finding the crag: From the parking area follow the steep main trail. At 0.3 mile is a junction with the Mishe Mokwe Trail to your right; continue on the main trail toward Sandstone Peak. At 1.1 miles pass a side trail to the summit of Sandstone Peak; continue on the main trail. At about 1.4 miles you will encounter a steep downhill

Mount Olympus

David Meyers playing with
cobbles at Mount Olympus

section; Mount Olympus is the tower on your left as the trail flattens out. Follow a climber's trail to the cliff.

Mars, 5.11b

The second route in from the left on the west face, which faces the main trail. Begin under a steep bulge. Weave your way up to the bulge, where you face the crux of the route, then follow cobbles to the anchors. 5 bolts to 2 open shuts.

Venus, 5.10b

This route climbs up next to the blunt arête on the west face. Start with a tricky boulder problem and finish up cobbles and over a small bulge. 4 bolts to 2 open shuts.

Up and Over Red, 5.11a

Scramble down to the spire's south side to access this route and Hercules. Start left of the huge bulge on the outside of the cave and follow steep cobbles straight up to the upper slab. 8 bolts to 2 rap hangers.

Hercules, 5.11c

This route starts just to the right of Up and Over Red and climbs through the cave with exposure right off the bat. Start left of the cave and make a stemming move off the pillar to get to the first bolt, then exit the cave onto a steep face with few rests. 10 bolts to 2 open shuts.

HUECO WALL

The Hueco Wall is a small satellite area that is great for lots of laps. The wall gets plenty of shade throughout the day and is safely bolted. The rock is of volcanic origin, and the climbing can be reminiscent of Malibu Creek. Most of the routes are about 45 to 50 feet long.

Finding the crag: Continue on the main trail from Mount Olympus. At 2.2 miles from the parking lot, the trail flattens out and comes to a junction with the Split Rock Trail to your right; take this trail. Shortly you will cross a dry creekbed. Follow the dry creek to the right and look for a climber's trail on your right in the bushes (there is an old water pipe across the trail where you enter). Follow this trail to two boulders; just before the boulders take a right onto the trail to the cliff. The top can be accessed by scrambling up around the left side of the wall.

Made in the Shade, 5.10c

The first route on the left side of the wall. Start in a groove at the base of the wall and make tricky moves up to and past the second bolt. The climb eases on big huecos to the anchors. 5 bolts to 2 open shuts.

Sudden Impact, 5.11a

Start 10 feet to the right of Made in the Shade under a small roof. Climb

Hueco Wall

One last lap on Red Devil (5.10c) at the Hueco Wall for David Meyers.

Jeff Willis discovered almost all the backcountry crags while trail running in the early 1990s. He used a stack of photos to convince Louie Anderson to follow him out there and see for himself that these crags needed to be bolted.

through the roof and trend slightly left, following good pockets and edges. After clipping the fourth bolt, head straight up to the anchors. 5 bolts to 2 open shuts.

Prodigal Son, 5.10c

The next route to the right. Start under the prominent black water streak and climb up through two bulges using tricky underclings to get past the second bolt. Follow pockets and flakes up the water streak to the anchors. 6 bolts to 2 open shuts.

Red Devil, 5.10c

This climb is up the small incline on the right of the cliff. Start on the right side of a huge rock protruding out of the wall. Make tricky moves to get on top of the protruding rock, then continue climbing on pockets and edges to the anchors in a huge hueco. 5 bolts to 2 open shuts.

Scar Tissue, 5.10a

The next route to the right of Red Devil. Start up another slight rise at the base of the wall and follow fun huecos and pockets. It's easy to miss the anchors; they are on the right just past the fifth bolt. 5 bolts to 2 open shuts.

Finders Keepers, 5.10a

This route starts just to the right of Scar Tissue and shares the same anchors. Weave back and forth following the weakest line of huecos and pockets. 5 bolts to 2 open shuts.

BONEY BLUFF

Boney Bluff stands out as the king of the backcountry—it boasts the highest concentration of hard, steep climbing in the Los Angeles area and the best view to boot. There are linkups in every direction you look underneath this giant crashing wave of pocketed volcanic breccia rock. The purest and most aesthetic lines at Boney Bluff are outlined in this guide. The pockets can be small and sharp at times, but are bullet hard. The bolts are close enough to work routes that are above your skill level, and the climbs get shade for most of the day. Most routes range from 25 to 50 feet long, and many have fixed draws.

Finding the crag: From the junction with the Split Rock Trail to the Hueco Wall, continue on the main trail and cross a dry creekbed on your left. Just after you climb out of the creekbed, look for a sign for the Backbone Trail on your left (also called Chamberlain Trail); follow this trail. At 2.7 miles from the parking area, you'll come to a junction with the Tri-Peaks

Isamer Bilog climbing high above the Pacific coastline on Piledriver (5.12b) at Boney Bluff.

Boney Bluff

Boney Bluff

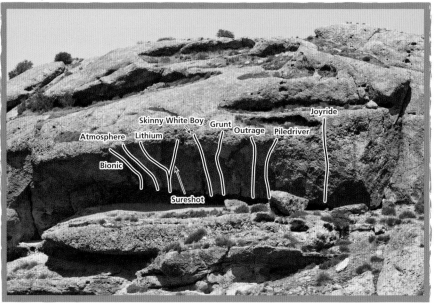

Trail; stay on the main trail and pass a sign saying "Entering State Park Property." Shortly after, you will see a faint climber's trail with rock cairns as markers on your right heading toward the obvious formation. Follow this trail uphill to the base of the cliff.

Bionic, 5.13b

The first full line of bolts on the left side of the wall (the lonely bolts to the left of Bionic are from an abandoned project). Start just left of the base of the major corner and climb through some large moves at the bottom to a cruxy mono move. 7 bolts to a 2-bolt anchor.

Atmosphere, 5.13d

The next line of bolts to the right of Bionic. Climb up a steep prow for three bolts and move left to the tricky bulge before the anchors. 7 bolts to a 2-bolt anchor.

Lithium, 5.13c

The next line of bolts to the right of Atmosphere. Climb to the second bolt, then continue up the left line of bolts to a sweeping prow with big moves on shallow pockets to the anchors. 7 bolts to a 2-bolt anchor.

Sureshot, 5.13b

This was the first route Louie bolted in 1995 when he began developing the crag. It shares the same start as Lithium. After clipping the second bolt, continue straight up the steep face to a crossover off a mono and some large moves to positive holds to the anchors. 6 bolts to a 2-bolt anchor.

Skinny White Boy, 5.12d

Start at the crack/dihedral in the middle of the wall. Positive holds lead to long pulls and a jump near the top off a bad pocket/pinch. 5 bolts to a 2-bolt anchor.

Grunt, 5.12c

The next line of bolts 8 feet to the right of Skinny White Boy. Start at two large pockets and climb to and past the large broken rail, making large moves and dynos between decent holds. 6 bolts to 2 open shuts.

Outrage, 5.13a

This route starts on top of a flat rock left of the big boulder at the base of the wall and is the left line of bolts. Use two large pockets to access the upper monos; the crux comes with a hard gaston move. 5 bolts to 2 open shuts.

Piledriver, 5.12b

Start on a flat rock just left of the big boulder at the base of the wall. Make some hard moves on small shallow pockets past the first bolt, then make a couple of long moves on positive holds past the crux below the anchor. 4 bolts to 2 open shuts.

Joyride, 5.11b

The third line of bolts left of the main arête on the right side of the wall. Use cheat stones to pre-clip the first bolt. A well-protected warm-up gets the crux out of the way early with shallow pockets that lead to more positive holds to the anchors. 5 bolts to 2 open shuts.

Angeles National Forest

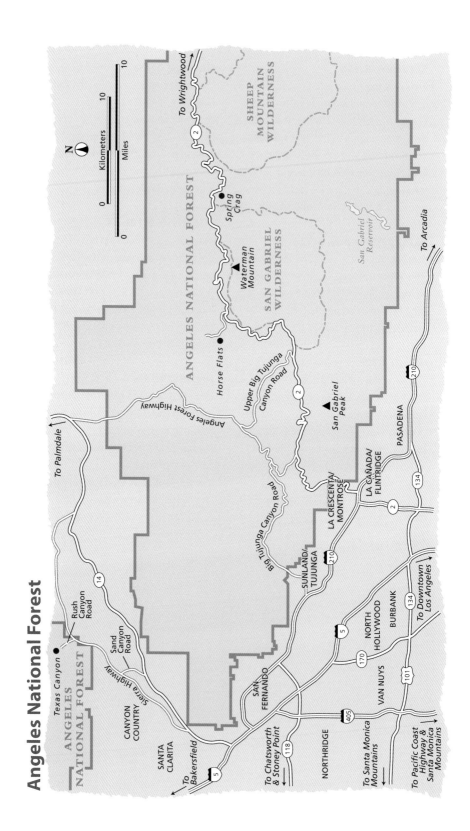

Angeles National Forest

It's a shame, but most Angelinos will go blank when you ask how to get to the Angeles National Forest. It is, however, one of the biggest "hidden gems" in LA County, with its 10,000-foot snowcapped peaks set against the backdrop of Los Angeles. With over 700 miles of hiking trails, 60-plus campgrounds, and 250 miles of OHV trails, the Angeles National Forest is an adventurer's paradise. In the summer of 2009 the Station Wildfire ripped through the forest, hitting brush that hadn't burned in over 150 years, causing over 160,000 acres of damage. For over a month firefighters fought to save the land, wildlife, and homes surrounding the forest. The forest has begun to regrow, but burn damage can still be seen all along the highways.

In 2005 the towering granite crag of Williamson Rock—hands down the best route climbing in SoCal—was closed to climbing due to the drop in numbers of an endangered species, the mountain yellow-legged frog. After the closure a group called the Friends of Williamson Rock formed; they have been working closely with the Access Fund, USDA Forest Service, US Geological Survey, and the US Fish and Wildlife Service to get climbing reopened at Williamson Rock. At the time of the closure there were only 5 to 10 frogs left in the area; currently there are over 150 documented frogs. The joint efforts of all these groups hope to provide seasonal access to the crag along with new trails and a pedestrian bridge over the stream where the frogs live. I'm hopeful that Williamson will be included in the next edition of this book.

When climbing in Angeles National Forest, you must display on your vehicle a national forest adventure pass, which can be purchased at any 7-11 or gas station near the entrance of the forest. Both day and annual passes are available for a fee.

Texas Canyon

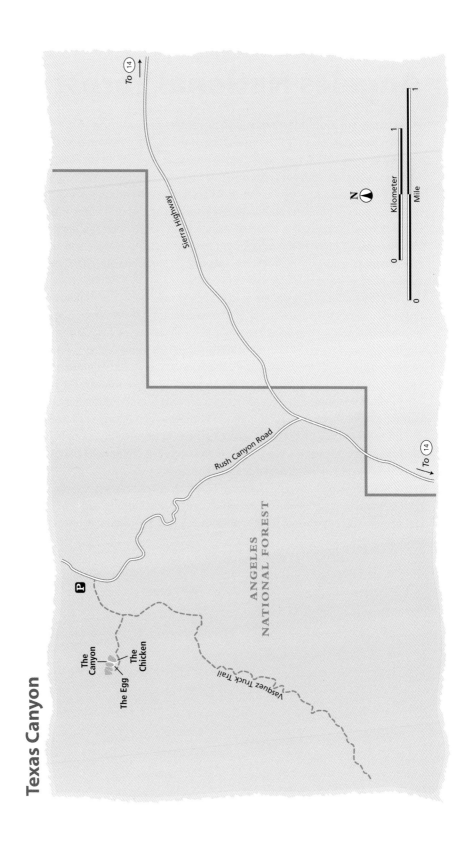

9.

Texas Canyon

Climbing started at Texas Canyon in the 1980s. Little is known about who put the first pieces of gear in, but in the early 1990s Scott Loomis bolted most of the harder routes, and Chris Savage followed in the late 1990s, bolting moderates at the crag. Development continues today on the outer formations.

The climbing at Texas Canyon is composed of sandstone conglomerate with long, runout slabs and more vertical climbs in The Canyon and The Egg. There are quite a few easy multipitch routes that can be led to the first anchors and then rappelled.

Primitive camping is allowed near Texas Canyon, although fires are prohibited. This is a very popular dirt bike and ATV area, so you may be disturbed by the noise at times. Since it is a dry desert area, please watch out for rattlesnakes. On your way out of town, stop by Bier Academy, at the corner of the Sierra Highway and Soledad Canyon Road, for amazing craft beers, specialty burgers, and sausages.

Getting there: From Los Angeles head north on either I-405 or I-5 to where they come to a junction in San Fernando. At 3.5 miles from the junction of the two interstates, follow signs for CA 14 North toward Palmdale/Lancaster. After 8.5 miles take exit 9 for Sand Canyon. Turn left onto Sand Canyon Road and follow it for 1.9 miles, then take a right onto the Sierra Highway. Take the Sierra Highway for 4.5 miles to a sign for the Rowher Flat OHRV area; turn left onto Rush Canyon Road here. After a short while the road turns to dirt, and at 1.6 miles you'll come to a pullout on the left-hand side where a gate blocks a fire road (Vasquez Truck Trail); park here.

Finding the crag: From the parking area walk past the gate onto the fire road and follow it for about 5 minutes to where a climber's trail leads off to the right toward the crag. Follow this trail for another 5 minutes.

THE CHICKEN
(AKA HYPERION SLAB)

There are many long and runout routes at The Chicken. Most of the routes are multipitch, but typically only get climbed to the first set of anchors.

Finding the crag: Walk down the main trail and head to the left side of the main crag. The Chicken will be in front of you.

Descent: For the multi-pitch routes, rappel down with two ropes for an easier descent, or use one rope to make multiple rappels to the base of the slab.

Endymion, 5.10b

Start on the left side of the main slab underneath a small curving roof with a big hole just above it. Climb thin holds on the lower slab to a crux move over the small roof and past the hole. Follow the bolts up easier terrain to a belay anchor at 80 feet. Rappel from here or continue up easy terrain for another two pitches to the summit. Pitch 1: 5 bolts to 2 bolted anchors. Pitch 2: 3 bolts to 2-bolt anchor. Pitch 3: Runout. 200 feet.

Aenea, 5.8

The next route to the right. Start up the slab and climb past the curving roof on its right side using pockets, cobbles, and edges to get past a reachy third bolt. The climbing eases and passes a small roof on its left before the anchors. 4 bolts to a 2-bolt anchor, 80 feet.

The Chicken (aka Hyperion Slab) and The Egg

Angeles National Forest became the first national forest in the state in 1908. It comprises over 650,000 acres ranging from low desert terrain at Texas Canyon to the high alpine peaks and pine forests at Horse Flats and Spring Crag.

Yellow Rose of Texas, 5.10b
The next route to the right climbs through the left side of the next small roof on the slab. Start up good terrain to clip a high bolt, then continue toward the left side of the roof. Use underclings and pockets to navigate past the roof and then climb slightly right before breaking off left to the same anchors as Aenea. 7 bolts to a 2-bolt anchor. 85 feet.

Hyperion, 5.7
The next route to the right. Start up the slab below the large roof and clip a high first bolt. The crux is pulling over the bulge using slopers and cobbles. Climb up and left on easier terrain to an anchor. Continue with easier climbing on cobbles and pockets to the summit. Pitch 1: 7 bolts to a 2-bolt anchor. Pitch 2: 2 bolts to a 2-bolt anchor. 200 feet.

Goldline, 5.6
The next route just to the right of Hyperion begins under the right side of the long roof and passes a small bulge for the crux. Climb cobbles up the slab to the anchors. Rappel from here or continue to the summit on easy terrain. Pitch 1: 5 bolts to a 2-bolt anchor. Pitch 2: 5 bolts to a 2-bolt anchor. 200 feet.

Pretty Good at Drinking Beer, 5.10c
Walk to the right around the slab to the tree growing next to the crag; begin just left of the tree on the slight overhang. Make some bouldery moves up to two large cobbles in the wall and then move up and right toward the large hole near the third bolt. Climb up the slab's right ridge to the anchors. 5 bolts to a 2-bolt anchor. 90 feet.

THE EGG

This little crag offers some excellent 5.10 climbing on shorter routes and steeper terrain than at The Chicken and Canyon. The Egg gets lots of sun, and the routes are about 50 feet long.

Finding the crag: The Egg is the formation to the left of The Chicken.

Slotterhouse, 5.10a

Start on the far left with a great vertical slot 5 feet up the wall. Climb up cobbles and edges past a large cobble in the slab. Make a few moves on the upper headwall to the anchors. 6 bolts to a 2-bolt anchor.

Texas Chainsaw Massacre, 5.10b

The next route to the right. Climb past two large cobbles and use pockets and knobs to the upper slab where you will need some proper slab technique to get to the anchors. 7 bolts to a 2-bolt anchor.

Boneyard, 5.10b

The next route to the right. Start climbing up pockets and edges toward large huecos and a giant cobble that leans to the right. Continue up small pockets on the slab to the anchors. 7 bolts to a 2-bolt anchor.

The Green Mile, 5.10d

This route is the farthest to the right and is the best line on the wall. Climb up the right-facing flake using pockets to get to the high first bolt. Climb past the bolt, trending to the right as the pockets get smaller on the upper wall to the anchors. 5 bolts to a 2-bolt anchor.

THE CANYON

This is the first major canyon between the formations at Texas Canyon and offers some shade throughout the whole day. There is a lot of climbing on the west wall of The Canyon that is not listed in this guide.

Finding the crag: From The Chicken follow the climber's trail up the gully between the formations.

Descent: For the multi-pitch routes, rappel down with two ropes for an easier descent, or use one rope to make multiple rappels to the base of the slab.

Tethy's, 5.7

The blunt left arête on the north end of the canyon. Hike all the way to the end of the corridor; the start is obvious at a left-leaning crack. Climb past this and follow the slab up the line of bolts, then cross a seam to access the upper slab and arête. Climb left of the arête on cobbles and pockets to the belay anchors. Rappel from here or continue up and left to the summit via easy terrain. Pitch 1: 6 bolts to 2 bolted chains. Pitch 2: 4 bolts to 3 chains. 180 feet.

Middle Earth, 5.9

As you walk north down the corridor toward Tethy's, the canyon narrows just below a very large cobble sticking

The Canyon

out of the wall—this is where Middle Earth begins. Start to the right of the large cobble and climb through two bolts to the lower-angle slab. Climb toward a large depression in the wall with a set of bolts on the left, then continue up and left to a large cobble protruding from the wall, where you will find the anchors. Rappel from here or continue up to the summit on cobbles and pockets. Pitch 1: 9 bolts to 2 chains. Pitch 2: 5 bolts to 3 chains (same anchor as Tethy's). 160 feet.

Pick Pocket, 5.7
This route starts about 40 feet to the right of Middle Earth. It is the second route to the left of the large water runnel that is Agua Negra. Climb to the first bolt, which is shared with Itsy

Crystalyn Falk earns the "vista increíble" near the top of Agua Negra (5.9) at Texas Canyon.

Bitsy Spider, and head left up the slab on good pockets and cobbles past the first three bolts to a bulge. Climb left to a distinct gray cobble and an anchor. Rappel from here or continue on cobbles up and left to the same anchors as Tethy's and Middle Earth. Pitch 1: 3 bolts to a 2-bolt anchor. Pitch 2: 6 bolts to a 3-chain anchor. 130 feet.

Itsy Bitsy Spider, 5.10a

This route starts 10 feet to the right of Pick Pocket, and heads straight up to climb on the outer left edge of the water runnel. Climb the low-angle face on good pockets past four bolts, then move left into the crux with technical pockets and footwork. Head back to the right after the fifth bolt over the bulge and to the anchors. 7 bolts to a 2-bolt anchor. 80 feet.

Agua Negra, 5.9

This route climbs up the middle of the pocketed water runnel in the center of the wall just left of a large tree. A low crux leads to fun climbing. Move to the right after the fourth bolt before the bulge and continue left on large cobbles to the anchors. 4 bolts to 2 chains.

Spider's Line, 5.5

Start about 15 feet to the right of Agua Negra, just right of the large tree. Climb up the low-angle slab to the right following three bolts. Once you get to the ridge, start climbing left toward the anchors; continue on easier terrain to the summit for a runout second pitch. Pitch 1: 4 bolts to 2 chains. Pitch 2: 4 bolts to chain anchors. 180 feet.

Horse Flats

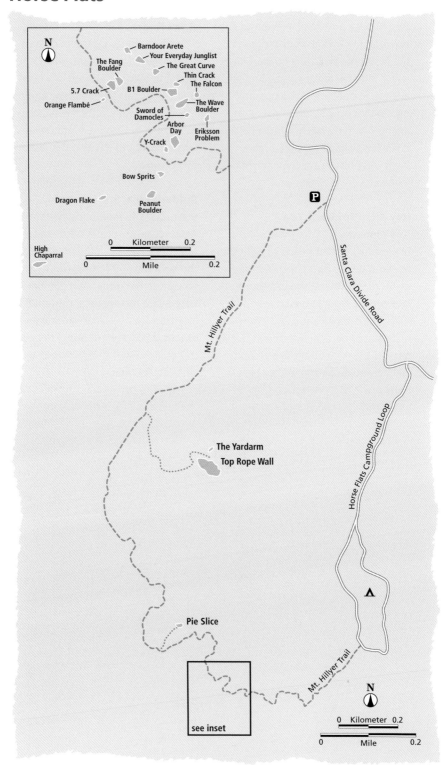

N

Barndoor Arete
Your Everyday Junglist
The Fang Boulder
The Great Curve
Thin Crack
5.7 Crack
B1 Boulder
The Falcon
Orange Flambé
The Wave Boulder
Sword of Damocles
Arbor Day
Eriksson Problem
Y-Crack
Bow Sprits
Dragon Flake
Peanut Boulder
High Chaparral

0 Kilometer 0.2
0 Mile 0.2

P

Santa Clara Divide Road

Mt. Hillyer Trail

The Yardarm
Top Rope Wall

Horse Flats Campground Loop

Pie Slice

Mt. Hillyer Trail

N

see inset

0 Kilometer 0.2
0 Mile 0.2

10.

Horse Flats

The landscape changes dramatically as you drive along CA 2, leaving the bustling city and heading into the alpine setting of Horse Flats. At 6,200 feet in elevation it's characterized by huge granite boulders flanked by towering Coulter and Jeffrey pines. Manzanita covers the forest floor where scrub jays, rabbits, rattlesnakes, bears, and deer run wild mere miles from downtown Los Angeles.

Climbing began in the early 1980s with a small crew of locals— Mike Paul, Mike Guardino, Matt Dancy, and Mike Ayon—who helped establish the majority of the easy to moderate plums. Erik Eriksson and Neal Kaptain joined in and put up some of the harder testpieces including the super technical Eriksson Problem. The area fell into the shadows once sport climbing at Williamson Rock started developing—until 1992, when James March visited the area and began a new flurry of development. Horse Flats now boasts some of the hardest and proudest boulder problems in Los Angeles County. Climbing ranges from short and powerful to tall and scary; the holds consist of perfect slopers, crystals, patina edges, flakes, and cracks; and there is something for everyone's style.

Fee camping at Horse Flats Campground (picnic benches and pit toilets) is available. Fires are allowed in the campground stoves when restrictions are not in effect. A gate near Angeles Crest Christian Camp on the way in closes at the first snowfall of the season and reopens on or around April 1 each spring. Temperatures are usually perfect for climbing in the early morning and late afternoon during the summer. Spring and fall are the best times to climb here, but if you are willing to make the extra walk (or bike ride) from the closed gate, winter can also be one of the best times of the year at the Flats. Make sure to stop by Newcomb's Ranch on your way in or out of the forest; they have a great selection of beers on tap and some good hearty bar food. The bar is 2 miles before the turnoff for Sulfur Springs/Santa Clara Divide Road.

Getting there: From the north take I-210 west or east and exit at CA 2 North toward La Cañada Flintridge. From the end of the exit, drive toward the mountains for 28.5 miles. The drive into Angeles National Forest is slow and windy with lots of motorcyclists and bicyclists—please drive safely. Turn onto the first paved road on your left after passing Newcomb's Ranch Restaurant—Sulfur Springs/ Santa Clara Divide Road—and drive for 2.5 miles until you see the Horse Flats Campground entrance on your left. You can drive into the campground and pay for one of the twenty-six campsites so you can park your car close to the lower trail. The other option is to continue driving down Santa Clara Divide Road for 0.75 mile toward the Mount Hillyer Trailhead at Rosenita Saddle, a pullout on your left.

From the southwest take I-10 east toward downtown Los Angeles, then take the exit (on the left) for CA 110 North just before you reach downtown. Drive for 4.2 miles and take exit 26A (on the left) toward I-5 North (Golden State Freeway). In 1.6 miles take the exit on your right for CA 2 North and follow CA 2 for 7.7 miles to the exit for I-210, then follow the signs for I-210 East. Drive for about 1 mile and take the exit for CA 2 North toward La Cañada Flintridge. At the end of the exit, turn left and drive for 28.5 miles. Follow the directions above to find the parking areas.

Finding the crag: From the campground follow the trail next to campsite #9 into the forest. Hike this trail for about 0.75 mile to access the main area.

From the Mount Hillyer Trailhead at Rosenita Saddle, hike for 1.5 miles down to the main area, passing the junction with the Top Rope Wall climber's trail on your left at about 0.75 mile.

TOP ROPE WALL

Follow the Mount Hillyer Trail to where it intersects the climber's trail on your left at about 0.75 mile from the Rosenita Saddle parking. (The start of the climber's trail is before you reach two large boulders on the sides of the trail.) Take the climber's trail down and to the left for a few minutes to the top of the Top Rope Wall. There is some fun bouldering at the summit of the crag. To access the main wall, follow the climber's trail down to the left of the crag; this will take you right under the crag and to the classic Yardarm boulder problem. The main wall is just to the right of the Yardarm. The roped routes are about 50 to 60 feet long.

Left Slab Route 3, 5.8

This route is on the left part of the main formation. Climb up the wide crack on the right with some awesome liebacking on a slab, then move into a more vertical and wider crack. Traverse left along an undercling and then head up the final flake to the top. This route can be led with a standard rack with extra wide gear for the bottom. Bring gear for an anchor.

Ant Line, 5.11c

Lieback the main flake up and to the right to the undercling flake, then traverse right making some tricky moves to get to the next thin vertical crack system in a small dihedral. Climb this to the roof flake; a long reach up and left grants you access to the upper face with delicate footwork guarding

Top Rope Wall

Left Slab Route 3

Ant Line

Horse Play

Norman Montes plugs in his last piece of gear before gunning to the top of Horse Play (5.8) at the Top Rope Wall.

the top. This route can be led with a standard rack with some extra small gear for the undercling flake and dihedral. Bring gear for an anchor or sling the tree. This route is typically toproped—for good reason.

Horse Play, 5.8

The crack to the right of Ant Line. Start by scrambling to the base of the flaring crack. Climb up to a good rest where the wide crack ends and it gets thin for a few moves; the crack turns back into hands near the top.

This route can be led with a standard rack. Bring gear for an anchor or sling the tree.

Bat Flake Arete, 5.12a

This toprope route is on the huge block that sits in front of the main cliff on the right side. The start can be a bit reachy and tricky, but leads to great climbing once you are established on the arête. There are bolts on top for an anchor. Scramble up the backside to access the anchors.

Top Rope Wall

Bat Flake Arete

The Yardarm, V3

This ultra-classic boulder problem is just to the left of the main wall. Traverse right along the flake until you get to the largest part at the far right. Make a big move up and right, then bust another huge move up with your left hand to the top, match hands, and top out.

Top Rope Wall

MAIN AREA

The largest concentration of boulders is found here. James March and friends spent countless days exploring and developing this area in the early 1990s, and there are still more first ascents to be discovered. From the junction with the Top Rope Wall climber's trail and the Mount Hillyer Trail, continue walking south along the ridge for another 0.75 mile. Arrive first at the Fang area, which is right in front of you as you come down the trail. If approaching from the Horse Flats Campground, hike along the trail leading out near campsite #9 for about 0.5 mile uphill to access the first set of boulders near the Bow Sprits area on your left and the prominent Y-Crack on your right. Climbs are listed starting from the campground trail and hiking toward the Rosenita Saddle parking.

In the 1800s Horse Flats was a hideout for Tiburcio Vasquez's stolen livestock and gang of bandidos—you can see why the jumble of boulders that cover the hillsides here was a perfect spot to escape the eye of the law.

Main Area

Bow Sprits Area

This is a great spot for highballs ranging from easy to hard. Bow Sprits is an all-time classic for the area and a "must do."

Finding the boulders: As you make the final steep switchbacks up the main trail from the campground, you'll see the Y-Crack in the bushes to the right of the trail and a climber's trail leading down into the depression on the left with two large boulders—Bow Sprits and The Peanut. Hidden in the bushes on the right of the trail just before Y-Crack is the massive Arbor Day Boulder.

Main Area

Arbor Day

Arbor Day sit

Arbor Day, V5R

This massive overhang is found on the boulder hidden in the bushes to your right before you get to the Y-Crack. Start on the obvious edge at head height and make a couple of big moves out left, then work your way up the black streak. A V9 sit-start begins on the lowest holds; make some powerful moves to get to the starting jug. **Descent:** Hop down on the left side toward the back of the boulder.

Horse Flats gained mainstream popularity in the early 2000s when SoCal native Lisa Rands's eye-popping ascents of the mega-classic and proud lines Orange Flambé and Sword of Damocles appeared in her popular film *Hit List*.

Better Bold than Old (aka Chicken Wing), V2R

Just around the left corner of Arbor Day, start low on a big left-facing flake and make moves up and left on thin edges to the horizontal break, then traverse right to better patina. Climb straight up through the black streak to top out. **Descent:** Hop down to the left of the boulder.

Bow Sprits, V2

Bow Sprits is the obvious arête on your right as you walk down the left-hand climber's trail. Start standing with a bad high right hand and your left on the arête, then make a couple of long reaches to finish on amazing patina jugs. **Descent:** Downclimb off the backside.

Y-Crack, 5.9

Just to the right of the main trail, start at the base of a tall, left-leaning crack and climb up to where another crack splits off to the right, then continue straight up the main crack or climb right. **Descent:** Scramble down the backside.

Main Area

Better Bold than Old

Main Area

The Peanut, V7

Walk past Bow Sprits to the boulder at the bottom of the depression; there are many good warm-ups on this boulder. Walk around to the backside to find The Peanut. Start on the huge jug down low and make a long move to a right sidepull, then use good crimps on the left and top out.

Nothing But Sunshine, V9

Start the same as The Peanut but cross your right hand up to the first crimp and make a long move out left to a decent sidepull. Continue up and left on good crimps, a sidepull, and a thank-god jug.

Main Area

B1 Boulder

This large square boulder is a perfect first stop for anyone hiking from either direction. The boulder features a variety of climbing styles and difficulties.

Finding the boulder: From the Y-Crack continue up the trail, passing many moderates and warm-ups on your left and right. When the trail flattens out, make a sharp left turn just before you see the B1 Boulder on your right.

B1 Traverse, V4

Start on the far right side of the west face on good holds. Traverse left until you can make big moves up and left onto the huge patinas to the top. For a V6 variation, sit-start with your left hand on a small crimp and right hand on the sloping arête, then make a couple of hard moves to join the traverse. **Descent:** Scramble off the back of the boulder or downclimb the easy jugs.

Natasha Barnes using the final thin edges of the B1 Face (V2) at Horse Flats.

Main Area

Thin Crack left and right

B1 Face

B1 Face, V2

Around the corner to the left of the B1 Traverse is this technical and crimpy face. Start with your hands on a ledge to the left and traverse right, then grab the flexing flake and match (pull down, not out). Make a long move up and right to another flake, commit to the upper sloping edges, and high-step to the top. **Descent:** Scramble off the back of the boulder.

Thin Crack, V0

Stand-start on the big protruding flake and lock your way up the left-leaning crack; top out to the left or right. **Descent:** Downclimb the right side of the boulder.

Main Area

The Great Curve

The Great Curve, V6R

This boulder is located on a small rise 50 yards to the left of the B1 Boulder. Start on the blunt left arête and make a leaping move to a sloper, then continue along the arête to a sketchy mantle. **Descent:** Walk off the back of the boulder.

The Wave Boulder Area

THE WAVE BOULDER AREA

This area hosts some of the harder climbs at Horse Flats. There are also a variety of warm-ups on all the boulders.

Finding the boulders: From the B1 Boulder walk down the little gully to the right; the Wave Boulder is the big, long boulder on your right. The Sword of Damocles is down to your right as you wrap around the Wave Boulder. The Eriksson Problem is on the left opposite the Sword of Damocles.

Blank Generation, V9

This is the major overhang that you first approach on your hike around the Wave Boulder. Start with your left hand on a good right-leaning flake and right hand on a flat crimp in the middle of the face. Make a huge move up and left to the lip and top out. Start matched on the flake to make it V10.

The Wave, V1

Just around the corner to the left of Blank Generation is an exposed, juggy overhang. Start on flakes and under-clings, climb left to make a long move to the lip, then match this and make the sketchy mantle.

The Wave Boulder Area

The Falcon

The Falcon, V5

This boulder is at your back when facing Blank Generation. Sit-start on the large rail and make a big move up and right. Keep the tension and move your left hand up to the sloping side-pull and top out.

The Wave Boulder Area

The Wave Boulder Area

Sword of Damocles, V8R

Just down the hill from The Wave is this imposing highball. Get established in the middle of the blank overhanging face and make a balancy move to the right arête. Find bad holds on the face for your left hand while bumping up the arête, then leap for the top. **Descent:** Scramble off the back of the boulder down the tree.

Eriksson Problem, V7

Just across the gully from the Sword of Damocles is this technical highball face. Start high on a razor edge for the right hand and a bad crystal for the left. Make tricky and balancy moves up knobs and more crystals to the top. **Descent:** Scramble down the side of the boulder.

The Fang Area

Orange Flambé

THE FANG AREA

This area features a variety of moderates and the beautiful face of Orange Flambé.

Finding the boulders: From the B1 Boulder continue up the main trail to the obvious 5.7 Crack on your right; the Orange Flambé boulder is on the left side of the trail down the slope slightly.

Orange Flambé, V8R

Begin on the west face of the boulder down at the base of the slope. Climb the beautiful, tall, orange face on technical edges, trending up and to the right at first, then straight up to top out.

5.7 Crack, 5.7

Climb the slabby crack, lieback the end, and make a long reach to the lip. **Descent:** Drop down over the backside or continue up and left on the next boulder and scramble down the notch.

The Fang, V3

Continue past 5.7 Crack and follow its slab up and around the right to the backside to a large overhanging roof with a distinct "fang" hanging off near the end. Start hanging on The Fang and use double heel hooks to work your way up the arête on the left, then use slanting face holds to the top. For a V6 variation, start down in the cave as for Zach's Roof and climb into The Fang.

Zach's Roof, V5

Start low in the cave with a right-hand sloping dish and a left-hand sidepull. Climb up the overhanging feature, eventually getting to a sloping right-hand hold, then climb up and right through good crimps to the top.

The Fang Area

5.7 Crack

The Fang

Zach's Roof

The Fang sit

Natasha Barnes taking a sunset cruise on The Fang (V3) at Horse Flats.

The Fang Area

Barndoor Arete, V2

This boulder is just to the north of The Fang. Climb the balancy and blunt arête—it only feels like a V2 after you have done it.

Your Everyday Junglist, V3

This climb is located on top of the large boulder to the right of Barndoor Arete. Use a flake as an undercling for both hands and make a move to small crimps, then make a big move to the top. For a V6 variation, start sitting on small crimps and make a hard move into the underclings or a large move to the small crimps above.

DRAGON FLAKE AREA

This area features a couple of beautiful highballs in a secluded area.

Finding the boulders: From the 5.7 Crack head down the gully toward Orange Flambé. Follow this faint climber's trail through a short corridor of boulders, then trend to the left and around a large formation. You'll hike into a faint canyon and soon see the top of Dragon Flake.

Dragon Flake, V5

This problem is on the west face of the boulder. Climb up the left-leaning crack for a few moves, then span right to a flake. At the end of the flake, make a long move up to a good hold on the arête, then top out to the left. **Descent:** Scramble down the backside of the boulder.

Dragon Flake Area

Dragon Flake

Dragon Flake Area

High Chaparral

High Chaparral, V5

Look for the pink face of High Chaparral up the hill to the west. Start low on the broken edges that face left. Make a hard move to a small edge up and left, then climb the technical face past a horizontal break. **Descent:** Downclimb off the side of the boulder.

PIE SLICE WALL

This wall offers a couple of toproping options on the right (5.10s) and the bolted sport climb Pie Slice; there is also some good bouldering around the base of the wall.

Finding the crag: From 5.7 Crack, continue hiking up the main trail for about 0.3 mile until you pass a rock formation on your left. The trail then makes a sharp right-hand turn; look for a climber's trail to the right leading toward the large Pie Slice Wall. Routes are on the south face.

Pie Slice, 5.10b

Start up the left-leaning crack (use medium gear to protect the initial runout to the first bolt). Climb onto the headwall using thin edges and knobs to the horizontal break, then traverse to the right along the ripples toward the jugs at the end. 4 bolts to bolted anchors.

Pie Slice Wall

11.

Spring Crag

Spring Crag is a beautiful protrusion of orange-streaked metamorphic granite tucked in a canyon near the Islip Saddle on the Angeles Crest Highway. Although the road is just below the crag, it is not a highly traveled section and it adds to the feel that you are miles away from the city.

Tom Gilje was the first to visit the crag and envision the lines. The crag itself is fairly small, so development was limited to only a handful of routes, but for climbers itching to get on a rope at some higher elevation, this is the ticket. The canyon is sunny in the mid-afternoon but can be cold in the late afternoon. The routes are about 55 to 65 feet long.

The Pacific Crest Trail (PCT), the famous western long-distance trail, stretches 2,663 miles from the border of Mexico and California to the border of Washington and Canada. Islip Saddle is the PCT's 356-mile marker from the southern trailhead.

Getting there: From the north and east take I-210 west or east and exit at CA 2 North toward La Cañada Flintridge. At the end of the exit, drive for 40 miles into Angeles National Forest to just past Islip Saddle. Park at a large dirt pullout on the right before the left-hand turn at the base of a canyon. Look for an old rock wall and staircase with a handrail just past the large pullout. In the winter after the first snowfall, prepare for the gate at Islip Saddle to be closed until April 1; you can park here and walk 0.5 mile to the start of the trail and regular parking area.

From the southwest take I-10 east toward downtown Los Angeles, then take the exit (on the left) for CA 110 North just before you reach downtown. Drive for 4.2 miles and take exit 26A (on the left) toward I-5 North (Golden State Freeway). In 1.6 miles take the exit on your right for CA 2 North and follow CA 2 for 7.7 miles to the exit for I-210, then follow the signs for I-210 East. Drive for about 1 mile and take the exit for CA 2 North toward La Cañada Flintridge. Follow the directions above to the parking area.

Spring Crag

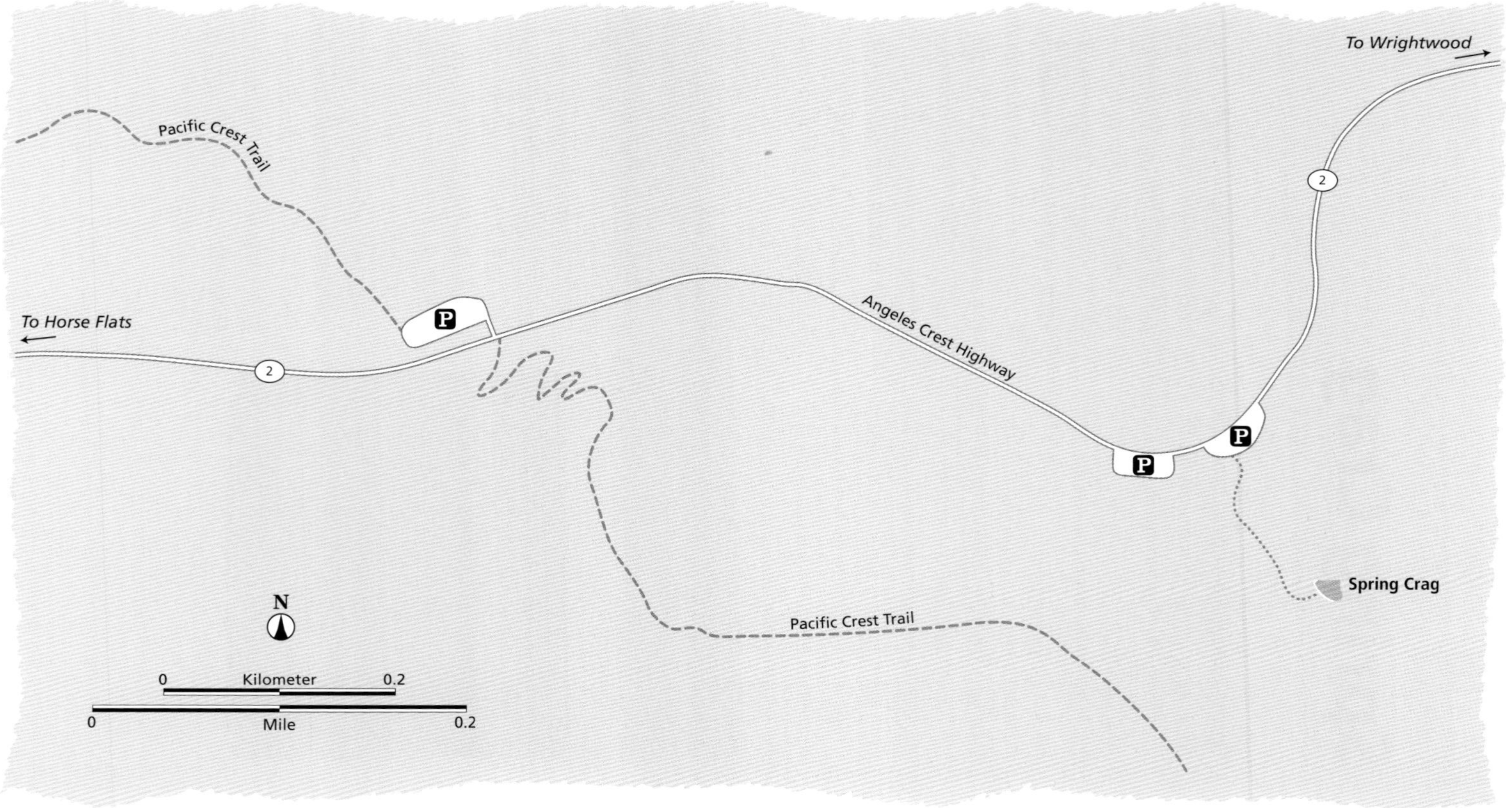

To Wrightwood

2

Spring Crag

Angeles Crest Highway

Pacific Crest Trail

Pacific Crest Trail

2

To Horse Flats

N

Kilometer
0   0.2

Mile
0   0.2

Isamer Bilog finds the last warmth of the sun on a rare snow day in Los Angeles on Loose Nut (5.10d) at Spring Crag.

Finding the crag: From the parking area follow the staircase up into the canyon, then follow a faint climber's trail up and right as it ascends the steep hillside. Continue over logs and scree for 5 minutes, then cross the creekbed to your left just below the base of the crag.

Mount Up, 5.11c

This route is on the narrow prow facing down the canyon. Climb up the face using the arête on the right and the vertical seams running up the face. Make some tricky moves near the top to the anchors. 5 bolts to 1 chain and 1 bolt anchor.

Stripped Nut, 5.11a

The second set of bolts around the corner on the main wall. Start just left of the small roof. Climb through some tricky blocky holds to clip a high first bolt. Continue climbing up and right following the blunt corner to easier terrain to the anchors. 4 bolts to 2 chain anchors.

Mount Up

Loose Nut

Stripped Nut

The Bandwagon

The Bandwagon, 5.10b

This is an easier alternate start for Stripped Nut and takes a direct line up the middle of the wall. Start just to the right of the previous route and climb up through two bolts before you join Stripped Nut at its third bolt. 4 bolts to 2 chain anchors.

Loose Nut, 5.10d

The last route to the top on the right side of the wall. Start below the right-leaning crack and climb up the slightly overhanging wall on crimps and flat edges. Move up and right toward the crack, then make a few moves to the bulge and a tricky mantle. Finish up the left side to the anchors. 5 bolts to a 2-bolt anchor.

Echo Cliffs from the Mishe Mokwa trail

Appendix

Gear Shops
Adventure 16 Tarzana
5425 Reseda Blvd.
Tarzana, CA 91356
(818) 345-4266

Adventure 16 West Los Angeles
11161 W. Pico Blvd.
Los Angeles, CA 90064
(310) 473-4574

REI Arcadia
214 N. Santa Anita Ave.
Arcadia, CA 91006
(626) 447-1062

REI Northridge
18605 Devonshire St.
Northridge, CA 91324
(818) 831-5555

REI Santa Monica
402 Santa Monica Blvd.
Santa Monica, CA 90401
(310) 458-4370

Sport Chalet Burbank
201 E. Magnolia Blvd., #145
Burbank, CA 91502
(818) 558-3500

Sport Chalet La Canada
Two Sport Chalet Dr.
La Canada, CA 91011
(818) 790-9800

Sport Chalet Porter Ranch
19817 Rinaldi St.
Porter Ranch, CA 91326
(818) 831-9520

Sport Chalet Thousand Oaks
1350 N. Moorpark Rd.
Thousand Oaks, CA 91360
(805) 494-4058

Sport Chalet West Hills
6701 Fallbrook Ave.
West Hills, CA 91307
(818) 710-0999

Gyms
The ARC Climbing Gym
305 N. Santa Anita Ave.
Arcadia, CA 91006
(626) 294-9111

Boulderdash
880 Hampshire Rd., Ste. A
Thousand Oaks, CA 91361
(805) 557-1300

L.A. Boulders (LAB)
1375 E. 6th St., Unit 8
Los Angeles, CA 90021
(323) 406-9119

Rockreation West LA
11866 LaGrange Ave.
Los Angeles, CA 90025
(310) 207-7199

The Stronghold Climbing Gym
650 S. Avenue 21
Los Angeles, CA 90031
(323) 505-7000

Top Out Climbing
26332 Ferry Ct.
Santa Clarita, CA 91350
(661) 288-1813

Guide Services
(Southern California Area)
ATS Adventureworks, (626) 434-3636

On Rope Consulting, (310) 804-7303

Sierra Mountaineering International,
(760) 872-4929

Sierra Rock Climbing School, (760)
937-6762

Southern California Mountaineers
Association, www.rockclimbing.org

Vertical Adventures, (800) 514-8785

Wilderness Outings, (877) 494-5368

Hospitals
Exer Urgent Care
26777 Agoura Rd., Ste. 4
Calabasas, CA 91302
(818) 880-2225
9 a.m.–9 p.m. every day

Kaiser Permanente Woodland Hills
Medical Center
5601 De Soto Ave.
Woodland Hills, CA 91367
(818) 719-2000
24 hours

Los Robles Hospital and Medical
Center
215 W. Janss Rd.
Thousand Oaks, CA 91360
(805) 497-2727
24 hours

Malibu Urgent Care
23656 Pacific Coast Hwy.
Malibu, CA 90265
(310) 456-7551
9 a.m.–8 p.m. every day

Olive View UCLA Medical Center
14445 Olive View Dr.
Sylmar, CA 91342
(818) 364-1555
24 hours

Saint John's Health Center
2121 Santa Monica Blvd.
Santa Monica, CA 90404
(310) 829-5511
24 hours

Santa Monica UCLA Medical Center
1250 16th St.
Santa Monica Blvd, CA 90404
(424) 259-6000
24 hours

USC Verdugo Hills Hospital
1812 Verdugo Blvd.
Glendale, CA 91208
(818) 790-7100
24 hours

West Hills Hospital and Medical
Center
7300 Medical Center Dr.
West Hills, CA 91307
(818) 676-4000
24 hours

A motor powered glider cruises low over the ocean near Leo Carrillo.

Index

Sunset near the Santa Monica pier

About the Author

Damon Corso, a freelance photographer (as well as director, producer, and videographer) and writer, has been photographing and filming rock climbing professionals for the past ten years across the United States and Europe. His work can be found on the covers and in feature articles of a multitude of major magazines, such as *Climbing*, *Urban Climber*, *Deadpoint*, *Rock & Ice*, *Los Angeles Magazine*, and *Exercise & Health Magazine*. His work is also on display at the Museum of Photography in Bad Ischl, Austria. Damon currently lives in North Hollywood, California, where he spends a majority of his time searching the High Sierra for untouched granite boulders.

PROTECTING CLIMBING **ACCESS** SINCE 199

| JOIN US |
WWW.ACCESSFUND.ORG